Hollywood's Other Men

Also by Alex Barris:

The Pierce Arrow Showroom Is Leaking

Hollywood's Other Men

Alex Barris

South Brunswick and New York: A. S. Barnes and Company
London: Thomas Yoseloff Ltd

© 1975 by A. S. Barnes and Co., Inc.

A. S. Barnes and Co., Inc.
Cranbury, New Jersey 08512

Thomas Yoseloff Ltd
108 New Bond Street
London W1Y OQX, England

Library of Congress Cataloging in Publication Data

Barris, Alex.
    Hollywood's other men.

    Filmography: p.
    1. Moving-picture actors and actresses. I. Title.
PN1998.A2B36   791.43′0909′27   73-18863
ISBN 0-498-01428-2

PRINTED IN THE UNITED STATES OF AMERICA

To the memory of my mother,
who first got me hooked on movies

Contents

Introduction

Conflict being a basic ingredient of any form of drama, from Shakespeare to *Shaft,* it is necessary that the spectator be able to recognize readily the opposing sides in any dramatic confrontation and be able to identify with one side or the other. Some quirk of human nature prompts us to ally ourselves with the "good" side and against the "evil."

Hollywood, which sired the commercial motion picture and set a pattern of values that still survives today, long ago faced up to the problem of audience identification in what now seems a rather simplistic manner.

In the days of the early silent films, primarily "action" or Western stories, the visual identification of the representatives of Good and Evil was made unmistakably clear: the good guys wore white hats, the bad guys black. To make the distinction even more vivid, good guys (i.e., sheriffs, marshalls, peace-loving ranchers, or farmers) were usually clean-shaven. Bad guys (rustlers, cattle barons, mortgage foreclosers, et al.) had mustaches or, at least, several days' growth of beard. Good guys usually rode white horses, bad guys were on dark ones; good guys drank milk or, in cases of dire need, sarsparilla; bad guys swilled whiskey and usually let some of it slurp down their dirty chins.

It's possible, if one cared to do so, to construct some sort of defense of this ingenuous approach. The early films, running two or three ten-minute reels, had to compress so much detail into a short time that there was no time for the niceties, such as evolution of character, no spare frame of film to be wasted in sketching in the fine lines of a portrait or delineating the subtler aspects of a man's nature.

But, of course, the habit of instant identification and right-between-the-eyes symbols outlasted that pioneer era of filmmaking. When "talkies" came in, the Westerns—ever the staple of Hollywood action drama—continued to use the same obvious labels. The hero wore white, the villain black.

As movie making progressed, the symbols did become a shade less pronounced, audiences were trusted to be able to figure out where the values lay, villains were sometimes disguised—that is, given some human dimensions—so that viewers could enjoy the fun of figuring out which way the plot was going to twist or, in the case of mysteries, "whodunit."

The 1930s, however, ushered in a new movie phenomenon, the light romantic comedy, in which the conflict was not so much between good and evil as between two suitors for the hand of the heroine. This called for a different approach to the business of handy symbols and audience "identification." (That this sort of story existed long before, in plays or novels, is almost irrelevant: the movies reached—and had to satisfy—countless millions not heretofore addicted to theater or printed fiction.)

Yet another factor helped complicate the problem. Hollywood's star system had already been established and the public had already been trained to expect their favorites to behave in prescribed manner. "Little Mary" (known thus even before she was accurately billboarded as Mary Pickford) could do no wrong, could not be allowed to do or say anything that didn't fit the milky-white public image of "America's Sweetheart." Theda Bara was the Vamp. Valentino was the Shiek. Clara Bow was the "It Girl." Garbo was aloof.

With talking pictures, new stars appeared—with new public images, but with the same rigid adherence to the borders of that image once it was established. Janet Gaynor was ever demure, Wallace Beery was the diamond in the rough, Cary Grant was debonair, Gable irreverent and brave, Rosalind Russell witty, Deanna Durbin eternally virginal, Gary Cooper heroically taciturn, James Stewart incorruptible, and so on. "Type-casting" was the direct result of the establishment in the public's mind of these inflexible "personalities" of the movie stars.

(On rare occasions, a star could break away from the rigidity of his or her public image, and then with only a fair chance of scucess. After a decade of playing impeccable, articulate playboys, Robert Montgomery boldly took on the role of a psychopathic killer in *Night Must Fall*, and won acclaim. Bette Davis had to wage a long court fight and defy her studio before she was allowed to bite into some serious roles. Spencer Tracy's near-perfect track record was flawed in *It's A Mad, Mad, Mad, Mad, World* when he played a cop who turned crooked—a switch his fans found difficult to accept.

The evolution of the light romantic comedy, however, imposed a new burden on Hollywood script writers and filmmakers of the thirties. Having by now drilled into the public's consciousness the "public personalities" of the stars, scripts had to be devised to present these stars acceptably, repeatedly, and yet with minimal variation.

This was somewhat easier to do in action pictures. Errol Flynn could be swashbuckling whether he duelled Basil Rathbone or Ian Keith or John Sutton, whether the background was Elizabethan England or Phillip's Spain or Balaklava, whether Olivia de Havilland was playing Maid Marion or Lady Hamilton. Basically, this was still the old game of good versus evil, black against white, with only surface refinements added as audiences were deemed to have become more "sophisticated."

But the conflict in the light comedy had to take on a different shape. If the heroine was to be forced to choose between two suitors, these two must represent vividly different values. If the hero was a star—as, inevitably, he was—he had to be debonair, or incorruptible, or taciturn, or irreverent, or tough, depending on which star was to play the hero. Therefore, for contrast, and to let the audience in on the key, the Other Man had to be graceless, or corrupt, or fast talking, or devout, or weak—again depending on which star was to play the hero and, significantly, NOT initially on who was to play the Other Man.

Thus, during the thirties, another whole school of actors developed in Hollywood movies, the need for this second group created by the strictures already established by the star system and the studios' idea of how much an audience could grasp without becoming confused.

The reader will doubtless notice a kind of pattern in the titillating titles of many of these light comedies of the 1930s and 1940s—*My Favorite Wife; My Wife's Best Friend; Too Many Husbands; Guest Wife; He Married His Wife; Her Husband's Affair; Unfaithfully Yours*—all suggesting a kind of naughty approach to marriage and fidelity. In those days censorship, either overt or implied, was such that infidelity was not regarded as a proper subject for comedy. The next best thing, therefore, was to devise ways of hinting at it without arousing the wrath of either the Breen office or the various moralizing pressure groups around the country.

Consequently, we had Irene Dunne and Cary Grant almost divorced—or perhaps marrying someone else after the original spouse was mistakenly believed dead—but invariably ending up back where they started: together again. Thus did the eternal triangle thrive in the naive Hollywood comedies of a generation ago.

It is to the actors who completed these misleading triangles—Hollywood's Other Men—that this book is primarily dedicated; to them and to those other standard props of those comedies—the friends, funny or serious, the mock rivals, the born losers of heroines, the magnanimous who stepped aside in favor of the heroes, the friends who helped patch up lovers' quarrels, the buddies who bailed out intemperate stars or offered a shoulder for heroines to cry upon.

Happily, many of them carved out quite substantial careers for themselves, almost always losing the girl—but always getting another picture. Many of them went on to become leading men, stars whose public image then became as valid and firmly accepted as their predecessors' had been.

Too few of them were ever given the credit they deserved. They were the butts of glib jokes that fell trippingly from the lips of stars. Reviewers usually relegated them to the last paragraphs of critiques, where it was generally acknowledged they were "competent." They were regarded by movie fans of those days as "funny" or "dumb" or "crazy." Although many of them were damned good actors, rarely were they nominated for (much less given) Academy Awards.

They were not all the same or interchangeable. They were as distinctive as were the stars they supported. The success of the movies they made often rested as much on their shoulders as on those of the "box-office attractions" for whom they were foils or fools.

But they, like the stars, set a pattern that also survives today, even in the severely abridged world of Hollywood. The Ralph Bellamys and Jack Carsons and Cesar Romeros of one era made possible the Gig Youngs and Tony Randalls and James Coburns of another.

Hollywood's Other Men

1
The Ralph Bellamy Role

The primary function of the Other Man in Hollywood comedies of the thirties and forties was to make the leading man look not simply good but better.

This Other Man usually represented solid values—honesty, dependability, sobriety, solvency. The hero usually conveyed quite the opposite: he was often out of work, he was irreverent, he wasn't above ignoring or even bending the law. In the movie cliché of the day, he tempted our heretofore prim and respectable heroine to kick up her heels at convention, walk barefoot in the rain, drink champagne, and dance all night, even stick out her tongue at the town gossip. Invariably, the heroine fell in love with this dashing reprobate, inevitably she rejected all the solid social values represented by the Other Man and married the penniless, jobless, sometimes unscrupulous hero.

But all this was part of the joke, the escapism of movies. For in fact Irene Dunne, Claudette Colbert, Carole Lombard, and Rosalind Russell were no more real than the Cary Grants and Fred MacMurrays to whom they surrendered their fluttering hearts. They were celluloid Cinderellas, launched on wild, improbable escapades with unlikely but attractive leading men.

Therefore, the symbol of sanity and security must also be caricatured. The Other Man had to be uninspired, pompous, conservative, unshakably decent, and never, never consciously funny.

If the word *square* had meant in the mid-1930s what it has come to mean in more recent years, it would have been the perfect way to describe Ralph Bellamy—or, more accurately, to describe Bellamy's public image once director Leo McCarey cast him in the second male lead in *The Awful Truth*.

Bellamy was no newcomer to Hollywood. He had appeared in numerous films, most notably perhaps in *The Wedding Night*, supporting Gary Cooper and Anna Sten. In this somber drama, Bellamy played Fredrik, a brutish farmer who is chosen as Miss Sten's husband, even though she loves Cooper.

Later in his lengthy career, Bellamy appeared in four films as Ellery Queen, the brilliant amateur detective, and in many other pictures, serious and otherwise. In 1944, his performance in *Guest in the House* won high praise. And Bellamy reached still greater heights with his dazzling portrayal of Franklin D. Roosevelt in *Sunrise at Campobello*, first on Broadway, then in the film.

But it was in *The Awful Truth* that Bellamy set a style that was to be copied by others and repeated by himself in a number of films over a period of years.

Ralph Bellamy. The personification of the Other Man, complete with umbrella, briefcase, and dumb look. If Bellamy didn't invent the role, he certainly performed it to perfection, again and again.

With a script by Vina Delmar and guided by the gifted McCarey (who won an Oscar for his direction), Bellamy personified the all-American square, the simple-minded nice guy who was dependable, decent, and dignified—and who didn't have a hope in hell of winning the girl.

Bellamy's first appearance in the film is classic. Irene Dunne, in the process of divorcing Cary Grant, has just been urged by her aunt (Cecil Cunningham) to get out and meet some people. Moments later, the aunt leaves the apartment and bumps into Bellamy, in evening clothes and sing-

ing to himself: "Oh, give me a home, where the buffalo roam. . . ."

He is, we promptly learn, an Oklahoma rancher and oilman, in New York with his dear mother. The aunt steers him toward Irene and love (not the real thing, you understand) is soon in bloom. Grant, who has visiting rights to the family dog, stokes the flames of his estranged wife's new romance while laughing at the whole ridiculous idea of sophisticated Irene finding this rich hayseed attractive.

Bellamy's grasp of the role is flawless. He takes

The Awful Truth. Ralph Bellamy bores Cecil Cunningham and Irene Dunne with details of life in Oklahoma in this early scene from the classic screen comedy. (Columbia, 1937)

Irene to a night club and, egged on by the ubiquitous Cary, gets her to dance with him. That dance is a hilarious romp, the Oklahoma oilman's version of jitterbugging. In her apartment, Bellamy sings "Home On The Range," with Irene at the piano. When she harmonizes with him, he gleefully slaps her on the back, and when their sour duet is over he guffaws happily and boasts: "Never had a lesson in my life."

Bellamy's cold-hearted mother is suspicious of Irene's sincerity (and purity) from the beginning and when Bellamy is finally confronted with evidence of her perfidy (Grant *and* another man come running out of her bedroom) Bellamy's parting line is straight as an Arrow collar ad: "Well, I guess a man's best friend is his mother."

After Irene's fling with Bellamy is thus thwarted, she sets out to destroy Cary's new romance and, eventually, Irene and Cary end up in a coy bedroom scene, with only minutes left before their divorce is final. But curiously, the film viewed today seems to go downhill after Bellamy's pompous exit.

So ably did Bellamy convey the True-Blue-Harold qualities of the role that he was in demand for the next several years to do it over and over

Lady in a Jam. Ralph Bellamy's two-gun approach seems to be lost on Irene Dunne, who's much more interested in Patric Knowles. (Universal, 1942)

again, with only minor variations. He was the rival (square) suitor in *Fools For Scandal*, with Carole Lombard and Fernand Gravet. In *Carefree*, with Fred Astaire and Ginger Rogers, he was Ginger's fiancé who sent the moody Ginger to psychiatrist Fred, only to lose her. He was a moonstruck cowboy in *Lady in a Jam*, with Irene Dunne again, this time with Patric Knowles as the dashing hero. He was the dull, plodding detective in Trade Winds, with Joan Bennett and Fredric March.

He was the steady, reliable (losing) suitor in *Coast Guard* with Randolph Scott and Frances Dee. In *Flight Angels* he was the old faithful feet-on-the-ground supervisor who lost Virginia Bruce to the more glamorous Dennis Morgan. For a switch, he was a dentist in *Footsteps in the Dark*, with Errol Flynn and Brenda Marshall —the switch being that he turned out to be the murderer. But he was, until the revelation of his guilt, still the solid, square Ralph Bellamy.

He became such a stock figure as the square that in 1941 film critic Bosley Crowther, in the course of reviewing *Affectionately Yours*, with Merle Oberon and Dennis Morgan, added, almost as an after-thought: "Oh, yes—Ralph Bellamy

Hands across the Table. As if competing with Fred MacMurray for Carole Lombard weren't tough enough, they put Bellamy in a wheelchair for this one. But it didn't matter; you knew the blonde manicurist would go for the glamorous wastrel instead of the wealthy Bellamy. (Paramount, 1935)

19

Coast Guard. Even in a dress uniform, Ralph Bellamy had a way of looking inadequate, as Randolph Scott's smile almost suggests. (Columbia, 1939)

plays the stupid rival suitor, as usual."

That same year, Bellamy sort of topped his own remarkable record by parodying himself in *His Girl Friday*, a Howard Hawks remake of the Ben Hecht-Charles MacArthur hit, *The Front Page*. In this updated version, the reporter was made a female (Rosalind Russell) and her running battle with her editor (Cary Grant) was punctuated by periodic appearances by Bellamy as the square insurance salesman waiting in the wings for Russell to quit her job and marry him. Naturally, she ends up with Grant.

From the mid-1930s on, there have been a number of actors who might be regarded as the spiritual (or stylistic) sons of Ralph Bellamy.

One of the most reliable, and least heralded, was Dick Foran. He had been in films for a few years, usually lurking in the background behind Dick Powell (in *Cowboy from Brooklyn*) or Jimmy Cagney (in *Boy Meets Girl*), but it was in a serious picture, *The Petrified Forest*, that Foran was most successful as the left-in-the-lurch suitor.

The movie had Bette Davis, Leslie Howard, and Humphrey Bogart as stars, but Foran's low-key performance was nevertheless an important one. He represented precisely the stodginess and security from which Bette longed to escape, an escape made possible by Howard's later noble sacrifice of his own life.

In a lighter vein, Foran was one of Mae West's handsome props in the frothy comedy, *My Little Chickadee*, which starred Mae opposite the redoubtable W. C. Fields. Foran was also on tap (as Joan Blondell's second choice) in *The Perfect Specimen*, Errol Flynn's first attempt at comedy. Foran returned to setting up Dick Powell in a 1941 Universal musical called *In the Navy*, which also had Abbott and Costello. In 1945, Foran was the dumb husband of Claudette Colbert in *Guest Wife*, a comedy in which Don Ameche won the girl.

His long list of credits includes one more serious role: as the dull, plodding, loyal friend of the family in *Four Daughters*. This time, for a change, his patience paid off—he won Gale Page.

Foran's film career was schizophrenic. At the same time that he was so effectively playing Other Men in comedies and dramas, he was also doing a series of B Westerns and made quite a reputation as a singing cowboy. But perhaps his rich, true baritone voice was too good: by the Second World War he was twanged out of this field by the emergence of Gene Autry and Roy

His Girl Friday. This remake of *The Front Page* had reporter Hildy Johnson changed into a woman (Rosalind Russell) and Cary Grant as the double-crossing editor. Waiting interminably in the wings, to marry Roz, was square suitor Ralph Bellamy. (Columbia, 1940)

Cowboy from Brooklyn. The title referred to Dick Powell, who won Priscilla Lane despite the protests of loser Dick Foran. (Warner Brothers, 1938)

Guest Wife. Even though he's holding hands with Wilma Francis above, Dick Foran was married to Claudette Colbert in this film, but was dumb enough to loan her to Don Ameche. It was, however, all quite innocent. (United Artists, 1945)

My Little Chickadee. No Mae West picture was complete without at least one handsome young man hanging about. In this case, it's Dick Foran, and the tearful type on the left is Margaret Hamilton. But Mae's real co-star was W. C. Fields. (Universal, 1940)

Second Fiddle. Tyrone Power can afford to look re-laxed. No matter what Mary Healy is saying to Rudy Vallee, it's Power who will win the heroine (Sonja Henie) and Vallee who is the second fiddle. (20th Century-Fox, 1939)

Rogers. After the war, Foran continued to act in a number of forgettable films and, in time, went the way of B pictures.

In contrast, another actor who was first known as a singer hammered out a career for himself in Other Man roles, starting in the late 1930s. This was Rudy Vallee, radio's "Vagabond Lover" for a decade, during which time he had worked only occasionally in films (*The Vagabond Lover, George White's Scandals*) and usually in strictly singing roles.

But in 1939, he played second fiddle to Tyrone Power in an early Sonja Henie film called *Second Fiddle.* This may have given a hint of Vallee's potential to Preston Sturges, one of Hollywood's most inventive comedy directors. It was Sturges who next used Vallee in a Ralph Bellamy-type role. This was in *The Palm Beach Story*, in which Claudette Colbert, estranged from husband Joel McCrea, is romanced by a stuffy millionaire with the ridiculous (typically Sturges) name of John Hackensacker II—played by Vallee.

The following year (1943) Vallee appeared in *Happy Go Lucky*, a comedy with Mary Martin and Dick Powell, with only moderately successful results. In 1947, he appeared with Cary Grant, Myrna Loy, and Shirley Temple in *The Bachelor and The Bobbysoxer*, again playing a pompous square.

But it remained for Preston Sturges again to

Other actors of the thirties and forties followed the Bellamy lead in a less flamboyant way. They played the part straighter than Vallee usually did, but still with considerable ability.

Although he is generally remembered as king of the B Westerns, Randolph Scott played his share of Other Man roles. He was putty in the hands of Mae West in *Go West, Young Man*, with Warren William as his more dashing rival. He stood around in a sailor suit in *Follow the Fleet* while Fred Astaire won Ginger Rogers. He fought John Wayne for Marlene Dietrich twice, in *The Spoilers* and again in *Pittsburgh*—and lost both times. Scott came closest to the classic Ralph Bellamy role in *My Favorite Wife*, a 1940 version of the old one about the spouse believed dead who returns after years on a desert island —just as hubby is about to remarry. The stars, as in *The Awful Truth*, were Irene Dunne and Cary Grant.

Leif Erikson, known to television fans as the father in the "High Chaparral" series, has been in Hollywood films since the early 1930s, and he, too, had his fling at Other Manning.

He was with Jack Benny and Dorothy Lamour in *College Holiday* in 1936; again with Miss Lamour (and Johnny Downs) in *Thrill of a Lifetime* the following year. In 1938, he was Bing

The Palm Beach Story. No one wearing pince-nez ever won a girl in a movie. The kneeling suitor here is Rudy Vallee, but it's Joel McCrea who got Claudette Colbert. (Paramount, 1942)

cast Vallee in a good Other Man role. This he did admirably in *Unfaithfully Yours* (1948), with Rex Harrison and Linda Darnell. In this one, Harrison was a symphony conductor who suspected his wife (Linda) of having an affair with Vallee. Most of the action revolves around Harrison's wild schemes for revenge, but Vallee's stuffy, square presence helps make it all even funnier. Sturges used Vallee once again (1949) in *The Beautiful Blonde from Bashful Bend*, with Betty Grable and Cesar Romero, but with less happy results all around.

Vallee had a good square role once again in *So This Is New York*, which starred Henry Morgan. Then, after a long absence, he became a Broadway star again in the musical comedy *How To Succeed in Business Without Really Trying*. When this was filmed (1967) Vallee repeated his role of the stiff, stodgy tycoon who is outwitted by ambitious Robert Morse—a role for which Vallee had ample training in those earlier movies.

How To Succeed in Business Without Really Trying. After a long absence, Rudy Vallee scored a stage and screen hit in this musical, playing a slightly older version of a role he'd done many times before. (United Artists, 1967)

My Favorite Wife. Near-bigamy was a favorite Hollywood theme. In this comedy husband Cary Grant returned just in time to stop wife Irene Dunne from marrying Randolph Scott. (RKO, 1940)

Crosby's rival in *Waikiki Wedding*, and in 1941 he lost Paulette Goddard to Bob Hope in *Nothing but the Truth*. He came (unsuccessfully) between Rosalind Russell and Paul Douglas in *Never Wave at a WAC*, and between William Holden and Dorothy Lamour in *The Fleet's In*. He was even the Other Man in such lesser items as *Miss Tatlock's Millions*, with John Lund and Wanda Hendrix, and *My Wife's Best Friend*, with Anne Baxter and Macdonald Carey.

For all his Hollywood comedies, Erikson (like Bellamy) returned to the Broadway stage in a serious role to win new acting laurels. In the 1950s, he played Deborah Kerr's unsympathetic

husband in *Tea and Sympathy*, then repeated the role on the screen.

Patric Knowles, who one-upped Ralph Bellamy to win Irene Dunne in *Lady In A Jam*, also played Other Men in a number of films, ranging from action pictures to breezy comedies. He was the second male lead in *It's Love I'm After*, with Bette Davis and Leslie Howard, but he won Olivia de Havilland. He won her again (even though Errol Flynn was the star) in *The Charge of the Light Brigade*, and once more in another Flynn film, *Four's a Crowd*, which paired Flynn with Rosalind Russell.

But Knowles was straight Bellamy in *Monsieur*

Pittsburgh. Despite this cozy scene between Randolph Scott and Marlene Dietrich, it was John Wayne who was the hero of this melodrama. (Universal, 1942)

Beaucaire, with Bob Hope and Joan Caulfield, and again in *Kitty,* with Paulette Goddard and Ray Milland. His later films included *Band of Angels,* with Clark Gable and Yvonne De Carlo, and *Auntie Mame,* with Rosalind Russell and Forrest Tucker.

The actors mentioned so far (Bellamy, Foran, Scott, et al,) tended to stick pretty close to the basic square style, letting the laughs come from the apparent seriousness of their humorless posture.

But there was also what might be regarded as a subdivision of the Ralph Bellamy School, in which the Other Man was more obviously a buffoon. Not for one moment did moviegoers believe

that the heroine would end up with one of these silly gentlemen, so outlandishly unacceptable were they. Yet here, too, some first-rate actors labored and built solid careers by playing these bizarre fops and comic villains, slick snobs and sneering "society" fakers. Surely, some of these actors merit attention here.

Among the best were three Englishmen: Reginald Gardiner, Reginald Denny, and Alan Mowbray.

Denny, who went all the way back to silent films, played one of his first Other Man roles in the Norma Shearer-Robert Montgomery version of Noel Coward's *Private Lives.*

He was an amusing thorn in Nino Martini's

The Big Broadcast of 1938. The formidable W. C. Fields was one of the stars of this name-heavy musical. The stiff young man in the naval uniform is Leif Erikson, a Bellamy-type of the era. (Paramount, 1938)

My Wife's Best Friend. Anne Baxter and Macdonald Carey were the stars, Leif Erikson (right) was only a passing fancy. (20th Century-Fox, 1952)

Tea and Sympathy. Successfully transferred from the stage, this film had Leif Erikson as Deborah Kerr's unsympathetic husband and John Kerr as the insecure student. (MGM, 1956)

It's Love I'm After. Olivia de Havilland and Patric Knowles were the second leads in this comedy, which starred Bette Davis and Leslie Howard. But the film helped establish Knowles as a stuffy Other Man. (Warner Brothers, 1937)

side in *Here's To Romance,* and got briefly in the way of Charles Boyer and Margaret Sullavan in *Appointment for Love.* He was also in *Romeo and Juliet* and *Anna Karenina* and *Rebecca.* In the late 1930s he appeared in a chain of detective films as Bulldog Drummond. But his ability as a comedy actor also helped *Mr. Blandings Builds His Dream House, The Secret Life of Walter Mitty,* and *Around The World in 80 Days.*

Alan Mowbray's imperious manner made him an asset to many thirties comedies, from *My Man Godfrey* to *Topper.* He had a winning flair for suggesting a kind of phoniness easily seen through his surface snobbishness, as if he were impeccably dressed in wing collar and cutaway coat—but with a hole in his sock. He could be as unkind to royalty (*Mary of Scotland*) 'as he was to commoners (*The King and the Chorus Girl*), but audiences were amused by him because he was so transparently fraudulent.

Reginald Gardiner was the perfect English "silly ass" type. Never a serious threat to any movie romance, he nevertheless added fun to many of them by his presence and his way of delivering brittle, withering dialogue. He was on hand in *That Wonderful Urge,* with Tyrone Power and Gene Tierney. He traded insults with Monty Wooley and Gracie Fields in *Molly and Me,* and with Betty Grable and Victor Mature in *Wabash Avenue.* One of his funniest roles (and his screen debut) was as a mad policeman leading an invisible orchestra in *Born To Dance.*

But probably Gardiner's greatest role came in 1942 in *The Man Who Came to Dinner.* Long regarded as a kind of road company Noel Coward, he got the perfect chance to prove himself in this Kaufman-Hart farce, for the role he played—that of Beverly Carlton, globe-trotting, devastatingly witty playwright-actor—was clearly a spoof of Coward himself, and Gardiner played it brilliantly.

The ultimate caricature of the Other Man role was shaped by a German-born actor who made more than one hundred movies. He was Sig Ruman and he will probably be best remembered for his appearances in several of the Marx Broth-

Monsieur Beaucaire. Being shaved by Bob Hope may seem an ignoble fate for Patric Knowles, but it wasn't unusual for actors noted as Other Men. The disdainful onlooker at right is Reginald Owen. (Paramount, 1946)

Private Lives. This film version of the Noel Coward play had Norma Shearer and Robert Montgomery as stars. The Other Man (seen above) was Reginald Denny. (MGM, 1934)

On the Avenue. The avenue referred to is Park, which may account for all the stuffed shirts. It was really about a poor boy (Dick Powell) and a rich birl (Madeleine Carroll), so Alan Mowbray (left, above) never stood a chance. The angry man in the top hat is George Barbier, and the little man on the right has achieved eternal anonymity. (20th Century-Fox, 1937)

ers films: *A Night at the Opera, A Day at the Races,* and *A Night in Casablanca.* If one can imagine Groucho Marx having a rival (usually for the bejewelled hand of the wonderful Margaret Dumont) it was often Ruman. He also added to the gaiety of such other films as *Ninotchka,* with Greta Garbo and Melvyn Douglas, *To Be or Not To Be,* with Jack Benny and Carole Lombard, and *On The Riviera,* with Danny Kaye.

Of the American actors who fit into this second

Bellamy "school," three deserve special attention: Lee Bowman, Allyn Joslyn, and Jerome Cowan.

Lee Bowman seemed to have been born in white tie and tails and was forever waiting for Irene Dunne or Rita Hayworth or some other cinema heroine to get over this nonsense (the nonsense being a flirtation with Boyer or some other hero) and settle down. With that weak smile of his, he eventually acknowledged defeat —to Boyer (in *Love Affair,* with Irene Dunne)

Ever Since Venus. Alan Mowbray, left, played many a mock suitor and as many phony aristocrats. In this comedy (which starred Ina Ray Hutton) he's seen with another veteran supporting player, Fritz Feld. (Columbia, 1939)

or Melvyn Douglas (in *We Were Dancing*, with Norma Shearer) or Gene Kelly (in *Cover Girl*, with Rita Hayworth). He lost Virginia Bruce to Walter Pidgeon in *Society Lawyer* and Mary Martin to Allan Jones in *The Great Victor Herbert* and Claudette Colbert to Melvyn Douglas in *I Met Him in Paris*. He was a cad in *Having a Wonderful Time*, with Ginger Rogers and Douglas Fairbanks, Jr., and in some lesser films. But cad or playboy, weakling or nasty husband, Bowman was always convincing.

Allyn Joslyn, like Bowman, had a snobbish streak in him, but with no compensating warmth. He was always a lightweight menace, a meddling reporter, a cold-hearted lawyer, a dyspeptic and disapproving in-law. He sneered at Bing Crosby in *If I Had My Way* and at Frederic March in *Bedtime Story*. He was a sharp-tongued director in *No Time For Comedy*, with Rosalind Russell and James Stewart, and he parodied Lucius Beebe, the chronicler of the upper crust, in *Cafe Society*, with Madelaine Carroll and Fred MacMurray. Joslyn was best when he seemed uncomfortable and confused, staving off indigestion with

The Doctor Takes a Wife. The doctor is Ray Milland. The wife (by the end of the movie) is Loretta Young. The man in the middle, and eventually on the sidelines, is Reginald Gardiner. (Columbia, 1940)

one hand and surrender to insanity with the other.

It is some indication of Joslyn's abilities as a comedy actor that he played on Broadway the role of Mortimer Brewster in *Arsenic and Old Lace*—a role given to Cary Grant in the later film version.

Then there was Erik Rhodes, a fine comic actor who despite appearances in other films is remembered best for those occasions when he was a kind of Latin Ralph Bellamy to Fred Astaire. Rhodes was Fred's "rival" for Ginger

Rogers twice, in *The Gay Divorcee* and *Top Hat*, and nothing he did before or after has so endeared him to movie fans.

To round out this gallery of Bellamy types there is Jerome Cowan, who combined the snobbery of Lee Bowman and Alan Mowbray with the cruelness and impatience of Allyn Joslyn. Cowan was a total nonbeliever, a postgraduate cynic, a foe of romance, and in some cases a complete scoundrel. As early as 1937 he was looking askance at Fred Astaire in *Shall We Dance*. He scoffed at Robert Young and Dorothy McGuire in

Claudia and David. He was unsympathetic to Bette Davis and Robert Montgomery in *June Bride.* Everyone else in the world might have believed that Edmund Gwenn was really Santa Claus in *The Miracle on 34th Street*—but not Jerome Cowan.

It's probably true that screen writers rarely invent a line of dialogue with a specific (secondary) actor in mind, but one line in a movie with Jerome Cowan described him so perfectly that it's tempting to believe this was an exception. The movie was *So This Is New York* (screenplay by Carl Foreman from a story by Ring Lardner) and the line was delivered by Henry Morgan in the scene that introduced Cowan to the audience.

"He had a way of looking at you," said Morgan, speaking of his brother-in-law (Cowan), "as if you were a side dish he hadn't ordered."

That Wonderful Urge. Reginald Gardiner looks appropriately outraged at the realization that Gene Tierney prefers Tyrone Power. (Note: No hero would ever wear mittens.) (20th Century-Fox, 1949)

A Night at the Opera. The long-running "love affair" between Groucho Marx and Margaret Dumont was often given extra spice by the presence of that master mock-rival, Sig Ruman. (MGM, 1935)

Love Affair. This highly successful romance teamed Irene Dunne with Charles Boyer. The scene above indicates about how close Lee Bowman ever got to Miss Dunne. (RKO, 1939)

Cover Girl. Rita Hayworth may seem pleased enough with Lee Bowman, but it was Gene Kelly who brought out the best in her. Bowman was a born Bellamy: a loser. (Columbia, 1944)

The Wife Takes a Flyer. That's Joan Bennett and Franchot Tone ignoring the menace of the Third Reich as represented by Allyn Joslyn. (Columbia, 1942)

No Time for Comedy. James Stewart's gloom is wasted, as is Louise Beaver's disapproval. And Rosalind Russell is really kidding. The only one who's serious is Allyn Joslyn, a gem of a loser in this and other films. (Warner Brothers, 1940)

Cafe Society. Madeleine Carroll (above) and Fred MacMurray starred in this comedy, and Allyn Joslyn played a kind of Lucius Beebe character, a society gossip columnist. The regal lady at left is Jessie Ralph. (Paramount, 1939)

Claudia and David. Jerome Cowan holds forth while John Sutton looks amused and Dorothy McGuire uncertain. Her thoughts are really on Robert Young, who played the other half of the title. (20th Century-Fox, 1946)

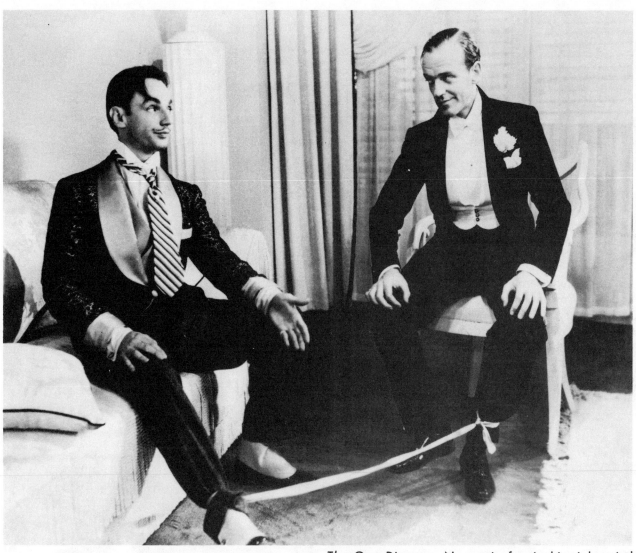

The Gay Divorcee. No movie fan in his right mind would believe for a moment that Erik Rhodes could offer serious competition to Fred Astaire for the hand (and feet) of Ginger Rogers, but he was the Other Man in this and another Astaire-Rogers musical, *Top Hat.* (RKO, 1934)

June Bride. Ex-war correspondent Robert Montgomery has just learned from his publisher (Jerome Cowan) that he's to work as an assistant to Bette Davis. Guess which one of them became a June groom. (Warner Brothers, 1948)

Guest in the House. The title refers to neither of these two gentlemen, Jerome Cowan and Percy Kilbride. But while Cowan had developed into a successful Other Man type, the man who more or less started it all had moved up to stardom in this drama: Ralph Bellamy. (United Artists, 1944)

So This Is New York. In humorist Henry Morgan's only starring film, Jerome Cowan (being socked by Virginia Grey) played the hero's detestable brother-in-law. (United Artists, 1948)

2
The Funny Friend

Often in the comedies and musicals of the first two decades of talking pictures, the hero of the story was blessed with a friend. Broadly, these "friend" roles could be divided into two subdivisions: the Funny Friend and the Nice Friend, although these categories sometimes overlapped.

The main duty of the Nice Friend was to step nobly aside at the appropriate moment, so the hero could get the girl. The function of the Funny Friend was simply to provide some laughs in the course of the film.

In both cases, of course, another job of the friend was to talk to or listen to the hero, so that we the audience could be privy to the plot without having to listen to a lot of boring soliloquies.

The Funny Friend sometimes got the hero into trouble, sometimes got him out of it. Sometimes he might appear to be part friend and part rival, but whatever the other characters in the story might pretend we knew he was never to be considered a serious rival for the girl.

Perhaps the most successful Funny Friend the movies ever developed was Jack Carson, the beefy, loud-mouthed but vaguely lovable second lead in dozens of films.

Carson had already been in films for several years before a hint of the Carson "image" began to shine through. The first good indication was in *The Bride Came C.O.D.*, a 1941 Warner Brothers comedy with Bette Davis and James Cagney.

Carson played a band leader whom heiress Bette decides to marry. Cagney is the pilot chartered to fly the lovebirds to Yuma to get married. But Cagney is bribed by her father to break up the marriage and, of course, eventually Cagney and Davis fall in love, leaving Carson with only his band to lead.

The following year, Carson had an even better part in *The Male Animal*, with Henry Fonda and Olivia de Havilland. This film, based on the Thurber-Nugent play, was a candy-coated plea for academic freedom, with a brash ex-football player pitted against a mild-mannered professor. Carson represented brawn while Fonda stood for brain and, naturally, intellect won over muscle-- thus demonstrating again the difference between reel and real life.

In 1944, Carson began what in time appeared like a full-time career as the Funny Friend of Dennis Morgan. First came a highly fictionalized biography of music-hall artists Nora Bayes (Ann Sheridan) and Jack Norworth (Morgan), titled *Shine On Harvest Moon*.

The team of Morgan and Carson worked so well that they subsequently appeared together in six more movies: *The Hard Way, The Time, The Place and The Girl, Two Guys from Milwaukee, Two Guys From Texas, It's A Great Feeling*, and *One More Tomorrow*.

Carson also played Funny Friend to Ronald

The Bride Came C.O.D. Only somewhere between the first and last reels Bette Davis switched her love from Jack Carson to James Cagney. (Warner Brothers, 1941)

Reagan, in *John Loves Mary*, to Rory Calhoun, in *Ain't Misbehavin'*, to Robert Cummings, in *Princess O'Rourke*, and to Fernando Lamas, in *Dangerous When Wet*.

Before his death in 1963, Carson had graduated to some leading roles (opposite Rosalind Russell in *Roughly Speaking* was a good example) and had even slipped into the role of Lucky Friend, a separate category to be examined in a later chapter.

Probably the next most popular Funny Friend in movies was Jack Oakie. The cheerful, apple-cheeked Oakie specialized in the broad double-take, often portrayed some show business types like song writers or agents, and never posed a serious threat to the romantic ambitions of stars like John Payne, Warner Baxter, Fred MacMurray, or Don Ameche.

Oakie represented the ineffectual point of the triangle with Payne and Alice Faye in such films as *The Great American Broadcast, Hello, Frisco, Hello,* and *Tin Pan Alley.* The last named was a kind of classic of its genre: the Hollywood musical about a pair of struggling tunesmiths, replete with the childlishly oversimplified insight into how hit songs are instantaneously created.

Although he started in films when sound came in, it was in the mid-thirties that Oakie's breezy, good-natured image came into focus. From *King of Burlesque*, with Warner Baxter and Alice Faye, he went on to *That Girl from Paris*, with Lily Pons and Gene Raymond, *Champagne Waltz*, with Fred MacMurray and Gladys Swarthout, and *The Toast of New York*, with Edward Arnold, Frances Farmer, and Cary Grant.

When first Sonja Henie and then Betty Grable challenged Alice Faye's position as queen of the 20th Century Fox musicals, Oakie was used as a funny friend in films with them: *Iceland* and *When My Baby Smiles at Me*.

By 1944, Oakie had slipped into such B musicals as *The Merry Monihans*, with Donald O'Connor and Peggy Ryan. Although he continued in films throughout the 1950s, his curiously 1930s appeal had waned and he was reduced to lesser roles in undistinguished movies doomed for the lower slot on double bills.

Equally successful in his own way was English actor Roland Young, the personification of meek, hen-pecked harmlessness. With a look that suggested the discomfort of mild constipation, Young underplayed his way through many comedies of the 1930s and 1940s.

Young was already an established stage actor

The Male Animal. Henry Fonda was the bookish professor, Olivia de Havilland his wife, and Jack Carson the beefy ex-football star. (Warner Brothers, 1942)

It's a Great Feeling. This time it was Doris Day with those same two guys, Morgan and Carson. Inevitably, Morgan got the girl, Carson the laughs. (Warner Brothers, 1949)

One More Tomorrow. Dennis Morgan and Jack Carson were almost as inseparable as Laurel and Hardy. The hungry doll is Alexis Smith, but the female lead was Ann Sheridan. (Warner Brothers, 1946)

Princess O'Rourke. Jack Carson was Robert Cummings's funny friend in this comedy, with Olivia de Havilland in the title role and Jane Wyman evening things up. (Warner Brothers, 1943)

A Star Is Born. In a rare dramatic role, Jack Carson was the cynical publicity man in Judy Garland's last great film. The man roughing him up is James Mason, who played Judy's has-been husband. (Warner Brothers, 1954)

Tin Pan Alley. Jack Oakie and John Payne were the song-writing team in this one. It wasn't important who wrote the words and who wrote the music. What mattered was who got the girl: Payne. (20th Century-Fox, 1940)

in London before he crossed the Atlantic (and the United States) and began acting in silent films. One of his first roles was in the Other Man category, as the overtrusting husband of Jeanette MacDonald in *Don't Bet on Women*, with Edmund Lowe as the more dashing alternative. (Note that in these terms, the Other Man need not be an interloper; he can be a husband. The point is that he is the loser.) But for a time Young played in dramas and melodramas, appearing twice as Dr. Watson to John Barrymore's Sherlock Holmes. He also made an impression as the

unctuous Uriah Heep in MGM's 1935 version of *David Copperfield*.

His greatest fame came in the title role of *Topper*, as Billie Burke's husband. This was the Thorne Smith fable in which Cary Grant and Constance Bennett played ghosts who kept getting in Topper's way. This was so successful that it led—inescapably, given Hollywood's greedy habit of squeezing blood out of every pebble—to two follow-ups. First was *Topper Takes a Trip* (with Grant appearing only briefly) and then *Topper Returns,* now with Joan Blondell and

Dennis O'Keefe replacing Grant and Bennett. (When a television series based on *Topper* was made, the Young role went to Leo G. Carroll.)

But Young was successful in other comedies as well. He was Katherine Hepburn's indulgent uncle in *The Philadelphia Story*. He was part of a family of charming rogues (again married to Billie Burke) in *The Young in Heart*, with Janet Gaynor and Douglas Fairbanks, Jr. He was aboard for laughs in *He Married His Wife*, with Joel McCrea and Nancy Kelly, and in *Two-Faced Woman*, with Greta Garbo and Melvyn Douglas.

In his later years, Young played a murderer in *The Great Lover*, a Bob Hope comedy, and was with Fred Astaire in *Let's Dance*. He died in 1953.

Young's American counterpart was Edward Everett Horton, one of Hollywood's most beloved comedy actors. Himself a master of the double-take, Horton refined it to suit his own fluttery personality. Horton probably uttered the word *Oh* more times than any other actor in movie history, infusing it with a broad range of meanings, from mild irritation to surprise to sly understanding to shock—and somehow managing to make them all funny.

King of Burlesque. That startled look on Jack Oakie's face may not have fooled Alice Faye, but it amused millions of movie fans in dozens of films. (20th Century-Fox, 1935)

Horton was in two early Astaire-Rogers musicals: *The Gay Divorcee* in 1934 and *Top Hat* a year later. He added a light note to the otherwise serious *Lost Horizon*, with Ronald Colman, Jane Wyatt, and Margo. He was right at home in *Bluebeard's Eighth Wife*, with Gary Cooper and Claudette Colbert.

One of his warmest roles was in the 1938 comedy-romance, *Holiday*, with Katherine Hepburn and Cary Grant. Here, Horton was a mildly absent-minded professor (married to Jean Dixon) whose friendship helped give Grant strength to stick to his anti-establishment guns.

Among his other distinguished screen credits were *Here Comes Mr. Jordan*, with Robert Montgomery and Claude Rains, *The Magnificent Dope*, with Henry Fonda and Don Ameche, *I Married an Angel*, with Jeanette MacDonald and Nelson Eddy, and *Arsenic and Old Lace*, with Cary Grant and Josephine Hull.

Horton, a shrewd theatrical trouper, enjoyed returning to the stage from time to time. When he was past his prime as a movie Funny Friend, he found a play called *Springtime For Henry*

Topper. Cary Grant and Constance Bennett were the two happy spirits in this famous comedy, and the man they "haunted" was Roland Young. (MGM, 1937)

The Philadelphia Story. Roland Young was Katherine Hepburn's likable uncle. In between them above are John Haliday, Mary Nash, and Virginia Weidler. (MGM, 1940)

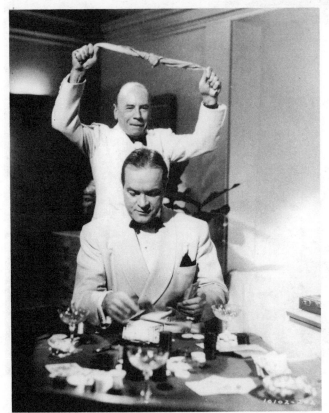

The Great Lover. In one of his last roles, Roland Young played a murderer in this Bob Hope comedy-with-intrigue. (Paramount, 1949)

The Gay Divorcee. Edward Everett Horton, here whispering in Alice Brady's ear, spent a lifetime being Funny Friend to just about everybody. In this instance, he was Fred Astaire's friend. (RKO, 1934)

Lost Horizon. Shangri-La wouldn't have been the same if Edward Everett Horton hadn't been on that planeload of outcasts who discovered a hidden civilization in Tibet. With Horton here are Ronald Colman and John Howard. (Columbia, 1937)

Bachelor Daddy. Betty Furness listens to Edward Everett Horton, while Raymond Walburn and Donald Woods look skeptical. Woods was a leading man in many B pictures, like this one, but in A films he was usually a rival/loser. (Universal, 1941)

See Here, Private Hargrove. The private's (Robert Walker) wish for privacy isn't respected by Keenan Wynn in this scene from the wartime comedy. (MGM, 1944)

Neptune's Daughter. Only Esther Williams could have been the star of a film with such a title. Her leading man was Ricardo Montalban, and Red Skelton was in charge of comic relief, ably assisted by Keenan Wynn, above, right. (MGM, 1949)

(which had been filmed in 1934, but without him) and spent many a summer touring in that time-tested comedy. He was eighty-one when he died in 1970.

The son of veteran stage and radio comedian Ed Wynn used to complain sometime, with mock bitterness, about his relative anonymity. He is Keenan Wynn and it was his lament that he was billed last in so many films that people thought his full name was "And Keenan Wynn."

He knew better, of course, for he has had a long and successful career—mostly playing Funny Friends to a string of stars.

Whereas Horton and Young usually portrayed mild-mannered, self-effacing characters, Wynn was blustery, loud, and superficially menacing. He first drew attention in the wartime comedy *See Here, Private Hargrove*, with Robert Walker in the title role. This was followed by the inevitable sequel, with Walker elevated a couple of notches, *What Next, Corporal Hargrove?* (One might be forgiven for feeling grateful that Marion Hargrove never made sergeant.)

A third film with Walker was *The Clock*, in which Judy Garland starred—and Walker (unlike Hargrove) was a sergeant.

In 1946, Wynn was the comic support of Van Johnson in two films: *No Leave, No Love*, with Marie Wilson; and *Easy To Wed*, with Esther Williams. Wynn appeared in two more Esther Williams underwater epics: *Texas Carnival*, with Howard Keel, and *Neptune's Daughter*, with Red Skelton.

Wynn appeared in many more films, including *Song of the Thin Man*, with William Powell and Myrna Loy, *My Dear Secretary*, with Kirk Douglas and Larraine Day, and *A Hole in the Head*, with Frank Sinatra and Edward G. Robinson.

Like so many other comedians, Wynn longed to play dramatic parts and he had his shot at a few of them, with good results. In 1964, he was a paranoic killer in *Man in the Middle*, with Robert Mitchum and Trevor Howard. But his most successful serious role was as Bette Davis's loud, obnoxious, but devoted husband in *Phone Call from a Stranger*.

Another impressive actor who switched from Funny Friend roles to heavier parts was William Bendix, who first attracted attention with Spencer Tracy and Katherine Hepburn in *Woman of the Year*, in 1941.

He was a heavy the following year in *The Glass Key*, with Alan Ladd and Veronica Lake, but he turned to Ladd's big-hearted sidekick in *China*, with Loretta Young.

The Second World War brought Bendix some of his best roles, among them *Wake Island*, with Brian Donlevy, *Guadalcanal Diary*, with Lloyd Nolan and a large cast, and *A Bell For Adano*, with John Hodiak and Gene Tierney.

On the serious side, Bendix starred in *The Hairy Ape*, the Eugene O'Neill play, in which he appeared opposite Susan Hayward. Still more memorable was *Lifeboat*, Alfred Hitchcock's 1944 exercise in confined suspense, with Tallulah Bankhead and Walter Slezak. Bendix also played the title role in *The Babe Ruth Story*.

Like so many other men, he had his fling at playing Funny Friend in a musical, *Greenwich Village*, with Don Ameche and Carmen Miranda, and in *Sentimental Journey*, with John Payne and Maureen O'Hara.

It's perhaps noteworthy that when Groucho Marx made one of his infrequent film appearances without the rest of his brothers, Bendix played his sidekick. This was the 1952 lightweight comedy, *A Girl In Every Port*.

But, of course, Bendix will probably be best

Abroad with Two Yanks. William Bendix and Dennis O'Keefe were the two yanks, separated by Helen Walker. This trifling service comedy was made the same year in which Bendix earned raves in *Lifeboat*, opposite Tallulah Bankhead. (United Artists, 1944)

remembered for his 1949 comedy, *The Life of Riley*. When this was turned into a popular television series, Bendix was starred.

Another durable Funny Friend was William Demarest, an old pro whose career started with vaudeville and spanned the talking picture years and television, in the long-running series, "My Three Sons." (Note: In this series, he replaced the late William Frawley, another Funny Friend of early movies.)

After attracting some attention in *Mr. Smith Goes to Washington*, with James Stewart and Jean Arthur, and *Tin Pan Alley*, with Alice Faye and John Payne, Demarest started what was to be a lengthy and profitable association with Preston Sturges.

Demarest's first role for director Sturges was in *The Great McGinty*, with Brian Donlevy. He worked again under Sturges in *Sullivan's Travels*, with Joel McCrea and Veronica Lake; *The Lady Eve*, with Henry Fonda and Barbara Stanwyck; *Christmas in July*, with Dick Powell and Ellen Drew; *Hail the Conquering Hero*, with Eddie Bracken and Ella Raines; and *The Miracle of Morgan's Creek*, with Betty Hutton and Eddie Bracken.

A Girl in Every Port. Groucho didn't have Harpo or Chico this time out, but he had the considerable presence of William Bendix. The young lady, incidentally, is definitely NOT Margaret Dumont. (RKO, 1952)

These were Preston Sturges's greatest and funniest films and Demarest is the only featured player who appeared in all of them. Perhaps incidentally, Demarest did not appear in any of the later, less noteworthy Sturges pictures.

But Demarest was not a one-director actor. He also played Funny Friend roles in *Along Came Jones,* with Gary Cooper and Loretta Young, *Ridin' High,* with Bing Crosby and Nancy Olson, *The Perils of Pauline,* with John Lund and Betty Hutton, and other, less memorable pictures. The closest Demarest came to a serious role was as Al Jolson's friend-cum-manager in *The Jolson Story,* with Larry Parks and Evelyn Keyes.

Two more early Funny Friends were Frank McHugh and James Gleason, who were better known in the 1930s and 1940s than they are now.

McHugh dates back to the Warner Brothers musicals and comedies of those days and continued into the era of action films, which sometimes called for the presence of a genial sidekick.

He was in *Footlight Parade,* with James Cagney, Ruby Keeler, and Dick Powell. He was in Warners' version of *A Midsummer Night's Dream,* with all the usual WB stars.

His mildly silly grin and artificial laugh endeared him to audiences in *Swing Your Lady,*

The Lady Eve. The deadpan artistry of William Demarest (behind Henry Fonda) began to assert itself in this Preston Sturges comedy, which starred Barbara Stanwyck opposite Fonda. (Paramount, 1941)

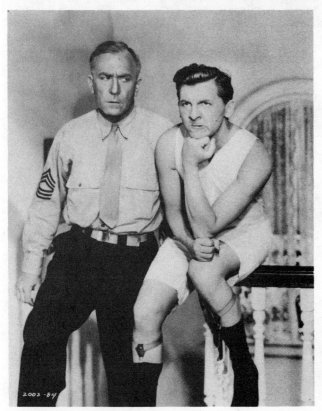

Hail the Conquering Hero. William Demarest's role in this satire on the wartime hunger for heroes was even bigger. The partially clad "hero" is Eddie Bracken. (Paramount, 1944)

The Miracle of Morgan's Creek. Demarest played Officer Kockenlocker, whose daughter (Betty Hutton) found herself pregnant without much recollection of how it happened. Eddie Bracken was her co-star. (Paramount, 1944)

Ziegfeld Follies. A table full of Funny Friends joined William Powell (who did a brief "guest" appearance) in this scene. From the left they are Slim Summerville, Frank McHugh, James Gleason, and Rags Ragland. (MGM, 1946)

State Fair. Frank McHugh consoles Dick Haymes in this scene from the Rodgers and Hammerstein version of an often-filmed story. The stars were Jeanne Crain and Dana Andrews. (20th Century-Fox, 1945)

My Son John. This McCarthy Era drama (starring Helen Hayes and Robert Walker) offered Frank Mc-Hugh the role of a friendly priest. (He had played a priest earlier in *Going My Way*). Walker, who was given to reading books, turned out to be a Commie spy. (Paramount, 1952)

Here Comes Mr. Jordan. James Gleason (second from left) was a Funny Friend to many a hero. In this fine comedy he was allied with Robert Montgomery. Flanking them are Don Costello and Benny Rubin. (Columbia, 1941)

a hokey yarn about a wrestling promoter, played by Humphrey Bogart; *Back Street*, with Charles Boyer and Margaret Sullavan; *Her Cardboard Lover*, with Norma Shearer and Robert Taylor; *Manpower*, with George Raft and Marlene Dietrich; *All Through the Night*, with Bogart and Peter Lorre; and *State Fair*, with Jeanne Crain and Dana Andrews.

One of his best roles, as a jovial priest, came in 1944 with the Bing Crosby-Barry Fitzgerald classic, *Going My Way*. And he was effective in the controversial (McCarthy-era anti-Red hysteria) *My Son John*, with Helen Hayes and Robert Walker.

James Gleason, a wiry, balding bundle of controlled rage, was the hard-boiled (but soft-centered) Funny Friend in countless comedies and comedy-dramas. In the mid-thirties, when "series" pictures were all the rage, he joined his wife (Lucille) and son (Russell) in a little Republic effort called *The Higgins Family*, but it didn't take.

Road Show. Bumbling, ineffectual Charles Butterworth brightened many films, even this minor wartime musical with Adolph Menjou and Carol Landis. The young lovely at his feet remains unknown. (United Artists, 1941)

Once Upon a Time. James Gleason peers at the caterpillar that was a focal point in this offbeat comedy with Cary Grant. (Columbia, 1944)

He was more acceptable in *Here Comes Mr. Jordan*, as the prize-fighter's manager; in *Meet John Doe*, with Gary Cooper and Barbara Stanwyck; in *A Guy Named Joe*, with Irene Dunne and Spencer Tracy; and in *A Tree Grows in Brooklyn*, with James Dunn and Dorothy McGuire.

Ever the tough-talking loyal friend, valiantly trying to steer the hero away from a disastrous course, Gleason worked with Cary Grant in *Once Upon a Time*, and with James Cagney in *Come Fill the Cup*. He also matched mock anger with Bendix in *The Life of Riley*.

Gleason's last film (he died in 1959) was as one of Spencer Tracy's lovable but obsolete political cronies in *The Last Hurrah*.

In a separate class among Funny Friends were Charles Butterworth and Robert Benchley.

Butterworth feigned a distracted air that always seemed to work. He appeared again and again in evening clothes, but somehow suggested he couldn't dress himself.

From the early 1930s (*Love Me Tonight*, with Maurice Chevalier and Jeanette MacDonald) to his death in 1946, Butterworth enlivened such romps as *The Moon's Our Home*, with Henry Fonda and Margaret Sullavan; *Swing High, Swing Low*, with Carole Lombard and Fred MacMurray; *Thanks for the Memory*, with Bob Hope and Shirley Ross; and *Let Freedom Ring*, with Nelson Eddy and Virginia Bruce.

In 1940's *Second Chorus*, Fred Astaire and Burgess Meredith vied for Paulette Goddard's favors, but Butterworth was also present as an inept, wealthy suitor and was the subject of one of the movie's songs, *Poor Mr. Chisholm*.

During the war years, he turned up in a series of inconsequential Andrews Sisters films like *What's Cookin'?* and *Give Out, Sisters*, plus such "all-star" revues as *Follow the Boys* and Irving Berlin's *This Is the Army*.

Robert Benchley was something of a Hollywood fluke. Already a noted humorist in print, he first gained movie fame in a series of shorts based on his own writings, including *The Treasurer's Report* and *How To Sleep*.

But Benchley's diffident manner appealed to audiences and he was used to good advantage

You'll Never Get Rich. Robert Benchley proved to be as funny on the screen as he was in print. Incidentally, Fred Astaire's dancing partner in this one was Rita Hayworth. (Columbia, 1941)

Ruggles of Red Gap. The Ruggles of the title was played by Charles Laughton, and Charles Ruggles (above, next to Laughton) lent staunch support, as did Zasu Pitts and Maude Eburne. (Paramount, 1935)

Collegiate. Joe Penner was the star but two Funny Friends helped garner the laughs: Jack Oakie and Ned Sparks. (Paramount, 1935)

in many films, most of them light comedies. He was with Robert Montgomery and Rosalind Russell in *Live, Love and Learn*. It was Russell again, with Brian Aherne, who got Benchley's support in *Hired Wife*. He aided Fredric March and Veronica Lake in *I Married a Witch*, and was with March again in *Bedtime Story*, with Loretta Young. Ray Milland and Ginger Rogers had Benchley's owllike presence in *The Major and the Minor*.

He also appeared in Hitchcock's wartime espionage melodrama, *Foreign Correspondent*, with Joel McCrea and Larraine Day; and in *Kiss and Tell*, with Shirley Temple.

Like Butterworth, Oakie, Gleason, and others, Benchley always pretty much played himself—which is exactly what the biggest movie stars have always done. No less so than with leading men, the men who played Funny Friends succeeded in establishing a public image that was

If You Could Only Cook. Herbert Marshall and Jean Arthur were the leads, but the spice was added by Leo Carillo, a familiar and welcome figure in many comedies. (Columbia, 1935)

likable, readily identifiable, and thus capable of being repeated again and again in an endless string of movies.

There were others, of course, who should not be completely passed over without mention: Charles Ruggles, who delivered every word of dialogue as if he were in doubt as to what the next word was; the aforementioned William Frawley, who made gruff stupidity a virtue; Billy Gilbert, the monumental sneezer; Arthur Treacher and Eric Blore, the epitome of gentlemen's gentlemen; Ned Sparks, the perennial sourpuss; Franklin Pangborn, the fussy hotel manager; Fritz Feld, the insufferably snobbish waiter; Leo Carrillo, who was everybody's Funny Friend, up to and including the Cisco Kid; and J. Carroll Naish, a masterful dialectician who alternated between funny character roles and menacing henchmen. The list could go on, but would soon slip a rung or two lower than the Funny Friends who stood as props for the Cary Grants and Ray Millands and Fred MacMurrays to play off.

One more Funny Friend, however, cannot be overlooked, if only because he was perhaps the most distinctive. He was Mischa Auer, Hollywood's all-time mad Russian, phoney aristocrat, irrepressible zany.

He was in several films, playing smallish roles, until 1936, when Gregory LaCava cast him in

Franklin Pangborn: A man with many hats, Pangborn was often seen as frazzled desk clerk, snotty hotel manager, unnerved banker, or punctilious tour guide.

This Could Be the Night. Jean Simmons and Anthony Franciosa starred. For J. Carroll Naish it was just another in an endless string of roles that made his face one of the best known in American movies. (MGM, 1957)

You Can't Take It With You. "Confidentially, it stinks!" was Mischa Auer's catch line in this fine Frank Capra film. With him above are Ann Miller, James Stewart, and Jean Arthur. (Columbia, 1938)

Mischa Auer: Starting with *My Man Godfrey*, the incomparable Mischa played eccentric Russians in a score of comedies, winning countless fans.

My Man Godfrey, an early zany comedy with William Powell and Carole Lombard. Auer's imitation of an ape was a masterpiece of irrelevant comic invention.

From then on he was in demand to perpetuate the mad Russian image he'd created. In Bing Crosby's *East Side of Heaven*, he wore a boxer's bathrobe marked "Moscow Golden Gloves—1919." He added much fun to two early Deanna Durbin films, *One Hundred Men and a Girl* and *Three Smart Girls*. He played what was left of the Danny Kaye role when *Lady in the Dark* was turned from a Broadway into a Hollywood hit, with Ginger Rogers and Ray Milland.

Auer's antics were seen in *It's All Yours*, with Madeleine Carroll and Francis Lederer; in *The Gay Desperado*, with Nino Martini and Ida Lupino; in *The Princess Comes Across*, with Carole Lombard and Fred MacMurray.

It was Frank Capra who best exploited what LaCava had started by putting Auer in *You Can't Take It With You*, in which he managed to stand out in a whole family of eccentrics.

Like most of Hollywood's Funny Friends, Mischa Auer eventually outlived his popular appeal, drifted into dreary second features (*Around the World*, with Kay Kyser) and smaller roles.

But Auer and all the others added spice and surprise to films for two decades and their contribution to the wide acceptance of hundreds of Hollywood comedies and musicals cannot be overstated. That they were funny is self-evident; that they were true friends—not only to the leading characters they supported but to the stars who played them—is something perhaps all the stars in question haven't fully acknowledged.

3
The Nice Friend

There is a story attributed to Jack Warner, one of the last of the movie moguls, about his reaction to the first reports that actor Ronald Reagan was considering trying for the presidency of the United States.

"No," cracked Warner, "that's wrong. It should be Jimmy Stewart for president—and Ronnie Reagan for Friend."

True or not, the story says something about not only Reagan's public image as a film actor but also the relative status of stars and lesser actors, or Friends.

Countless stars, from the 1930s to the present, have been blessed with on-screen friends, who served a variety of superficial functions but who, somehow, never got the girl. Even in scripts where they might be in love with the heroine they lost out.

Having examined the Ralph Bellamy role and the Funny Friend, the next category in this survey concerns itself with the Nice Friend, that stalwart, reliable, true-blue buddy (or mock rival) who usually made it through to the end of the movie, but was excluded from the final clinch. Sometimes, in a spasm of originality, the Nice Friend would be permitted the dignity of a dramatic death scene as a tidy means of clearing the field for our star. But dead or alive he was a foreordained loser.

As with those in other categories, the actor who played Nice Friends sometimes went on to play leading roles or serious rivals, but more often than not he became typed as a Nice Friend, doomed to nobly stepping aside in favor of the hero, or suffering in silence as the girl he loved blithely ignored his devotion. In less romantic roles, he merely stood by, helped the star solve his problems, and rejoiced in our hero's final triumph, whatever its nature.

Ronald Reagan started turning up in Warner Brothers pictures in 1937, generally playing leads in B pictures like *Love Is on the Air* and *Sergeant Murphy*. He had a lesser role in a 1938 Bogart film called *Swing Your Lady* and in *Cowboy from Brooklyn*, starring Dick Powell. In 1939, he was one of Bette Davis's cardboard playboys in *Dark Victory* and had similarly unrewarding roles in *Brother Rat and a Baby*, *Going Places*, and *Naughty But Nice*.

In 1941, the *Motion Picture Herald* surveyed movie exhibitors to choose from among the newer screen talent of the 1940–41 season the players they considered "Stars of Tomorrow." Reagan placed fifth on the poll, behind Larraine Day, Rita Hayworth, Ruth Hussey, and Robert Preston. That year he had achieved some sort of status in an Errol Flynn film called *Santa Fe Trail* by playing a man marked for martyrdom: George Armstrong Custer.

He did somewhat better in *Knute Rockne, All-*

Dark Victory. Drinking to forget her impending blindness is Bette Davis. The young man to the left of her is Ronald Reagan (in a small role) and next to him is Cora Witherspoon. (Warner Brothers, 1939)

American, which had Pat O'Brien in the title role. But Reagan's most impressive role was in *King's Row,* in which both his legs were amputated by a singularly insensitive doctor. When Reagan came to and realized his legs were missing, he looked down along the blanket and cried in horror: "Where's the rest of me?" (Years later, when Reagan, already in politics, wrote his autobiography, he titled it, *Where's the Rest of Me?*)

California's other ex-actor-turned-politician is George Murphy, who served six years in the United States Senate. Murphy was one of several dancers who became screen personalities, not quite as big as Fred Astaire and Gene Kelly, but certainly well known and in demand for some years.

Murphy's best years were spent playing Nice Friends. He was friend to Astaire in *Broadway Melody of 1940,* and dancing partner to Eleanor Powell in *Broadway Melody of 1938,* even though Robert Taylor was the romantic lead.

One of his biggest parts—and, in a way, the definitive Nice Friend role—was in *For Me and My Gal,* a 1942 musical-drama with Judy Garland

Kings Row. Ronald Reagan lost his heart to Ann Sheridan and his legs to an over-zealous surgeon in this highly successful drama. (Warner Brothers, 1941)

Broadway Melody of 1938. Eleanor Powell matched taps with George Murphy (above) but she saved her love for Robert Taylor. (MGM, 1938)

Broadway Melody of 1940. Nice guy George Murphy hears some bad news from Fred Astaire. The bad news might well have been that Astaire would win Eleanor Powell. (MGM, 1940)

and Gene Kelly. If only for its value as a classic cliché, perhaps the story of *For Me and My Gal* merits a closer look.

The movie was made very soon after the United States entered the Second World War and one of its functions was to serve as a kind of animated recruiting poster. It was a backstage story set in the First World War, liberally sprinkled with songs and directed by the famed Busby Berkeley, by then well past his peak of fame.

It starts with Judy Garland and George Murphy working together in smalltime vaudeville. George is clearly in love with Judy, but she treats him like a big brother. (She is working to put her real, and younger, brother through medical school.) Enter Gene Kelly as a brash, egotistical vaudevillian who immediately tries to lure Judy away from George, both professionally and personally. Judy can't stand Kelly and in the early

scenes they are forever sniping at each other—a sure sign, in Hollywood mythology, of true love.

Kelly succeeds in getting Judy to walk out on George, who takes the blow bravely, telling her (falsely) that he was planning to break up the act anyway. Soon, Judy knows she loves Gene, but he is as selfish as ever. When he gets a chance to join a bigger star (Marta Eggerth) he thinks nothing of ditching Judy—until he realizes, aided by appropriate off-camera music, that he loves her.

Just when Judy and Gene are set to open at the Palace, his draft call comes up. Kelly then commits an unpardonable act: he purposely injures his hand (with a trunk lid) to delay being drafted. Judy, whose brother has already been killed in the war, is appalled at Kelly's cowardly action.

"You'll never make the big time," she tells him, "because you're small time in your heart."

Remorseful, Gene now montages his way through all the branches of the armed forces, trying in vain to join up. But that mangled hand causes him to be rejected.

The scene shifts to Paris, where Judy is entertaining the troops. In the audience is ever-loving George, still in love with Judy. He goes backstage to see her and they plan to go out after the show. She asks him if he can wait and George, looking as mournful as a Nice Friend ever looked, says, "Sure. I'm a good waiter."

But Kelly suddenly turns up as another Y.M.C.A.-sponsored entertainer (you get the feeling that the First World War involved only these three people, plus extras) and Judy realizes she still loves him. It remains for Gene to perform some heroic act to prove he is no coward. The opportunity happily presents itself and Gene promptly destroys a German machine gun nest with some hand grenades that just happen to be lying about.

Having resolved such unpleasant matters pleasantly, we go to a final scene in which Judy and Gene, reunited, do a reprise of the title song while the hapless George grins good-naturedly as the camera moves past him for the closing two-shot of the stars. Such is the fate of a Nice Friend.

Murphy also stood by in *A Girl, a Guy, and a Gob* while Edmond O'Brien romanced Lucille Ball, back in 1941. In *Step Lively*, a rehash of

For Me and My Gal. Judy Garland and George Murphy may be smiling at each other, but it's Gene Kelly who's seated next to Judy, and that's the way it went. (MGM, 1942)

Room Service, he played a fast-talking producer, but the romantic leads were Frank Sinatra and Gloria DeHaven. Murphy made many more films than that—both with and without dancing shoes —but few in which he fitted so well into the category of Nice Friend.

If the plot of *For Me and My Gal* seems all too familiar it's only because it has been used so many times, particularly in the 1930s and 1940s, as the framework for musical films that purported to give us a glimpse of the backstage life of glamorous theatrical folk—vaudevillians, songwriters, producers, etc. It became such an overworked cliché that in 1973 a candy company used a capsule version of the story as the basis of a commercial. But in those halcyon days when movies were more naive and audiences more receptive, it was perfectly acceptable.

Even before *For Me and My Gal,* much the same basic plot had been used in 1938 for an especially successful musical from 20th Century-Fox. This was *Alexander's Ragtime Band* and

Alexander's Ragtime Band. The fiddling leader is Tyrone Power. Glumly at the piano is Nice Friend Don Ameche, who lost Alice Faye to Power. At the drums is Jack Haley. (20th Century-Fox, 1938)

Love Is News. Editor and reporter clash, perhaps because Don Ameche has just realized that Tyrone Power will again win the girl, Loretta Young in this case. (20th Century-Fox, 1937)

The Magnificent Dope. Don Ameche looks secure, despite Edward Everett Horton's apprehension. But it was the man on the magazine cover (Henry Fonda) who won the girl. (20th Century-Fox, 1942)

starred Tyrone Power and Alice Faye, with Don Ameche in the role of Nice Friend.

In this one, Alice is the band vocalist, Don is the piano player, and Tyrone, the leader, plays violin. Power is ambitious, Ameche loyal. When opportunity knocks, Alice and Don can't bring themselves to stand in his way—even though it means (gulp!) breaking up the act. Poor Don comes closer to winning than usual: he actually marries Alice. But, alas, we know her heart belongs to Tyrone, who eventually gets around to claiming it. Along the way, naturally, there are a couple of dozen Irving Berlin songs to be sung, and they helped make these films palatable, despite the dramatic predictability.

Ameche was a veteran Nice Friend and sometime Likable Rival. Besides *Alexander's Ragtime Band,* he lost Alice Faye to Tyrone Power in *In Old Chicago,* and in *Love Is News* he lost Loretta Young to Power. In *The Magnificent Dope,* he lost Lynn Bari to Henry Fonda.

In such films Ameche served his apprenticeship and eventually won what apparently was the supreme reward in Hollywood for a rising actor: scripts in which you get the girl. He won Betty Grable, Sonja Henie, and even Alice Faye in a succession of musicals, and won recognition as an actor for his portrayal of Alexander Graham Bell. From then on he was a leading man instead of a friend, for a good many years, until age eased him out of the triangle altogether.

Another example of an actor who served an apprenticeship as Nice Friend before graduating to stardom was Henry Fonda, although he did start at the top. After establishing his credentials on the stage, he went to Hollywood in 1935 to make his film debut, playing a leading role opposite Janet Gaynor in *The Farmer Takes a Wife.*

The following year he was starred along with Sylvia Sidney and Fred MacMurray in *Trail of the Lonesome Pine,* in which he was Sylvia's hillbilly suitor until city slicker MacMurray came along. The bitter rivalry between the two men —and that between two feuding mountain families—made this a fine picture. But in the end, Fonda lost Sylvia to Fred, thus qualifying as a Nice Friend/Likable Rival. (In *The Magnificent Dope,* mentioned earlier, Fonda as a country bumpkin won out over city slicker Don Ameche.)

In 1938, he was with George Raft, Dorothy Lamour, and Louise Platt in *Spawn of the North,* but the handy business of having two men and two women side-stepped the usual triangle problems. Next came *Jesse James,* with Tyrone Power in the title role and Fonda as his brother, Frank. As a rule, brothers in Hollywood films don't make out too well, and this one followed the rule.

The same year, Fonda was cast in *The Story of Alexander Graham Bell,* with Don Ameche in the title role. Fonda may have seemed wasted in that one, but in fact he was vital to it. Playing the role of Thomas Watson, Bell's friend and assistant, he had to be on hand when the inventor spoke that first historic sentence into the phone: "Watson, come here; I want you." Imagine where A.T. & T. would be now if Fonda hadn't been there.

In *Lillian Russell,* a highly fanciful biography of the noted star, Fonda was one of a squad of swains in pursuit of Alice Faye, who played La Russell. They included Edward Arnold, Warren William, and the ubiquitous Don Ameche. Fonda played Lillian's first husband, who was conveniently done away with to make room for Ameche.

But in the same year Fonda appeared in *The Grapes of Wrath,* one of the finest films ever to

The Trail of the Lonesome Pine. Fred MacMurray was the citified engineer and Henry Fonda was the inarticulate hillbilly. What they're fighting over is Sylvia Sidney, and Fred was the winner. (Paramount, 1936)

The Story of Alexander Graham Bell. Assistant Henry Fonda seems more excited than telephone inventor Don Ameche. Fonda was no rival here, just a Nice Friend. (20th Century-Fox, 1939)

Lillian Russell. Henry Fonda's romance with Alice Faye didn't last too long. After he was killed, she chose Don Ameche. (20th Century-Fox, 1940)

come out of Hollywood, and from then on he was accepted both as an outstanding actor and as a front-rank star.

One of the most durable Hollywood actors to spend years in the Nice Friend/Likable Rival pigeon-hole was Pat O'Brien, who in the space of six years made no less than eight films with James Cagney.

Hollywood discovered the "colorful" Irish (if, indeed, it didn't invent them) in the early 1930s. Cagney and O'Brien were first at each other's throats in *Here Comes The Navy,* in 1934. Next came *Devil Dogs of the Air.* Having conquered sea and air, Cagney and O'Brien got around to land fighting in 1940, in *The Fighting 69th.* In between came such titles as *Ceiling Zero* and *Angels with Dirty Faces* and *Torrid Zone* and even *Boy Meets Girl.*

O'Brien was doomed to playing second banana to Cagney—but always a nice one. When Cagney was a gangster, O'Brien was a cop or a priest. When Cagney was an unenthusiastic soldier, O'Brien was an inspiring Father Duffy.

Despite the insults they hurled at each other and the frequent fisticuffs, you knew they really liked each other and that sooner or later O'Brien would step aside to let Cagney have Olivia de Havilland or Ann Sheridan.

One of these confections was called *The Irish in Us,* and in a way it was the mold for many others. Cagney, O'Brien, and Frank McHugh are brothers, the Irish sons of an ever-so-Irish mother. McHugh is a fireman, O'Brien is a cop, and Cagney is a wastrel, who daydreams of managing a championship fighter. It's O'Brien who brings home his girl (Olivia) but it's Cagney she falls in love with, and the family is ripped asunder.

Cagney's current boxing protégé is a punch-drunk clown (played by Allen Jenkins) and on the night of the Big Fight he can't go on, so, naturally, his manager-trainer (Cagney) takes his place. He takes a terrible beating for several rounds, until O'Brien, swallowing both his pride and any hopes he may have had of winning Olivia, dashes to Jimmy's corner and guides him to a spectacular knockout victory.

As Edmund Lowe and Victor McLaglen had done earlier, and as Dennis Morgan and Jack Carson were to do later, Cagney and O'Brien specialized in presenting lovable, loving, scrapping rivals who played again and again the same stories (only the backdrops and the costumes changed) and always with the same result: Cagney won, nice guy O'Brien lost.

Among actors with a flair for comedy, few have

Flirtation Walk. Sergeant Pat O'Brien may look tough to rookie Dick Powell, but he's all heart. Of course, it was Powell who sang the love songs to Ruby Keeler. (Warner Brothers, 1934)

Devil Dogs of the Air. Margaret Lindsay looks sympathetically at Pat O'Brien, a sure sign that she'll end up with Cagney again instead of O'Brien. (Warner Brothers, 1935)

been as successful in portraying the Nice Friend as Eddie Albert, whose career has spanned three decades. (As recently as 1972, he again proved his ability by winning an Oscar nomination for his supporting performance in *The Heartbreak Kid.*)

Starting on Broadway in *Brother Rat* (and then in the film version), Albert has played friends (*You Gotta Stay Happy*, with Joan Fontaine and James Stewart) and rivals (*The Perfect Marriage*, with Loretta Young and David

Niven) and many comedy roles in between.

One of his best Nice Friend performances was in the outstanding romantic comedy *Roman Holiday*, in which Gregory Peck played a down-at-heels journalist who meets a runaway princess (Audrey Hepburn) and squires her around Rome. Albert was Peck's photographer friend, hired to take furtive pictures of the princess on a spree. Much of the fun came from Albert's attempts to keep up with Peck's frequent changes of tactics.

Torrid Zone. George Tobias holds a gun on James Cagney, Ann Sheridan, Pat O'Brien, Jerome Cowan, and Helen Vinson. In such moments of attack from outside, Cagney and O'Brien usually patched up their differences. (Warner Brothers, 1940)

The Irish in Us. Ever the nice guy, Pat O'Brien was good to his mother (Mary Gordon, above), introduced his girl (Olivia de Havilland) to his brother (James Cagney), and watched them fall in love. (Warner Brothers, 1935)

Till We Meet Again. In this remake of *One Way Passage,* Merle Oberon and George Brent were the doomed lovers and Pat O'Brien was the detective sent to bring Brent back. The other girl is Geraldine Fitzgerald, left. (Warner Brothers, 1940)

Meet Me after the Show. A chuck under the chin was all Eddie Albert got from Betty Grable. After the show she met Macdonald Carey. (20th Century-Fox, 1951)

Roman Holiday. Princess Audrey Hepburn says her farewells to newspaperman Gregory Peck and his Nice Friend, photographer Eddie Albert. (Paramount, 1953)

Carrie. In this truncated version of Theodore Dreiser's book, Jennifer Jones was first taken in by Eddie Albert, then by Laurence Olivier. (Paramount, 1951)

Albert also had his serious side, as evidenced in *Carrie*, a watered-down version of the Theodore Dreiser classic in which he played a breezy traveling salesman who lures Jennifer Jones astray before Laurence Olivier appears on the scene to lead her further astray.

But for the most part, Albert specialized in comedy roles, usually as a Nice Friend or Likable Rival and almost always abiding by the basic rule that prohibits nice friends from ending up at the altar.

Another Hollywood veteran who spent a lifetime playing Nice Friends was Walter Brennan, the first actor to win three Academy Awards: in 1936 for *Come and Get It*, with Joel McCrea and Frances Farmer; in 1938 for *Kentucky*, with Loretta Young and Richard Greene; and in 1940 for *The Westerner*, with Gary Cooper. (As of 1973, he is still the only three-time Oscar winner among actors.)

In all of these, as in many more pictures, Brennan was the twangy, earthy, tobacco-juice-spitting friend of the hero. In *Banjo on My Knee* it was Joel McCrea again. In *Stanley and Livingstone* and *Northwest Passage* it was Spencer Tracy. And besides *The Westerner*, he made three other films with Gary Cooper: *Sergeant York*, *Meet John Doe*, and *Pride of the Yankees*.

Come and Get It. Nice Friend Walter Brennan looks on as Edward Arnold and Edwin Maxwell shake hands. Joel McCrea and Frances Farmer starred. (United Artists, 1936)

For a time, it looked as if Brennan was going to do a state-by-state portrait of Nice Friendliness. Besides the aforementioned *Kentucky*, he was in films titled *Maryland, Home in Indiana, Dakota*, and *Return of the Texan*.

Quite different from Brennan, yet just as consistent in playing Nice Friends and likable sidekicks was Thomas Mitchell. And his list of credits is almost as long and impressive as Brennan's.

It includes such outstanding films as *Gone with the Wind* (as Scarlett O'Hara's father) and *Lost Horizon* and *Our Town*. Mitchell's irreverent manner, coupled with a lyrical, almost poetic approach to speech, made him an asset to every film he worked in.

He rarely played a rival. Perhaps the closest he came was in *Mr. Smith Goes to Washington*, in which reporter Jean Arthur, rejected by James Stewart when he realizes she has been exploiting him, turns briefly to Mitchell and even agrees to marry him. You know how long that notion lasted.

Mitchell won an Academy Award for his portrayal of a boozing doctor in *Stagecoach*, the classic John Ford Western. He made an effective rabble-rouser in the Charles Laughton version of *The Hunchback of Notre Dame*, and he supported Henry Fonda in *The Immortal Sergeant* and Gregory Peck in *The Keys of the Kingdom*.

For some years, he was in that group of favorites that John Ford liked to use in his films. Besides *Stagecoach*, Mitchell worked for Ford in *The Hurricane* and *The Long Voyage Home*. And Frank Capra, who had cast him in *Lost Horizon* and *Mr. Smith Goes to Washington*, employed him again for *It's a Wonderful Life*, with James Stewart and Claudette Colbert, and in *A Pocketful of Miracles*, with Glenn Ford and Bette Davis. That one, in 1961, was one of his last films. He died the following year.

No Hollywood star had a more loyal Nice Friend than Van Heflin, another busy actor from the early 1940s on. Typical of his roles was that in *H. M. Pulham, Esquire*, in which he was friend to Robert Young. Although he was in love with Ruth Hussey, he stood quietly by while she married Young.

In *Johnny Eager*, supporting Robert Taylor and Lana Turner, he was gangster Taylor's unswerving buddy and cried his way into a supporting actor Oscar for 1941.

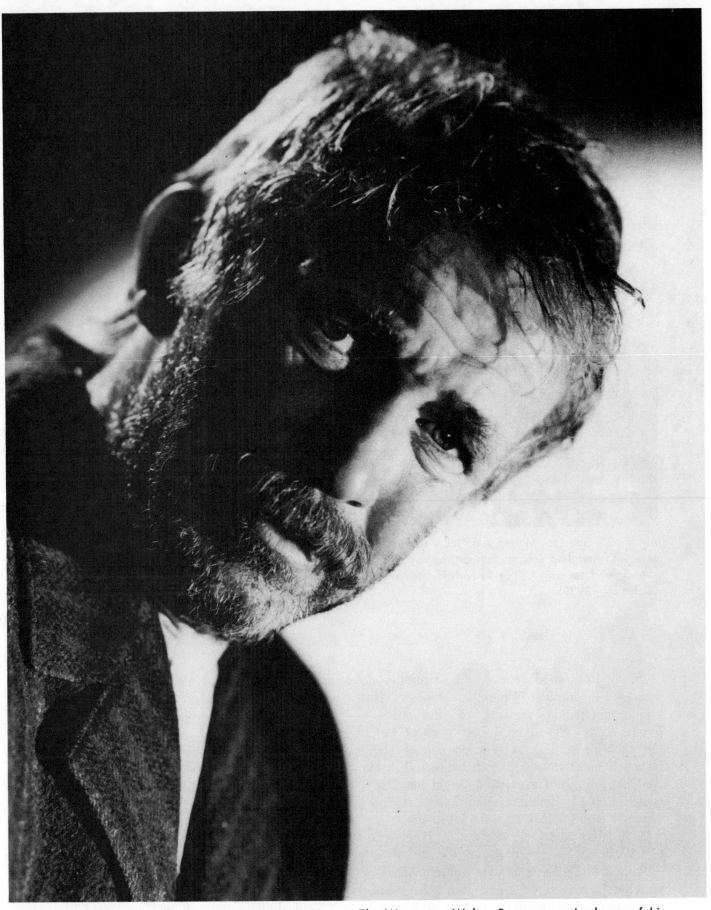

The Westerner. Walter Brennan received one of his three Oscars for portraying Judge Roy Bean in this Gary Cooper picture. (United Artists, 1940)

Mr. Smith Goes to Washington. Jean Arthur fell in love with fledgling senator Stewart, but at one point she agreed to marry Nice Friend Thomas Mitchell. (Columbia, 1939)

During Hollywood's era of making massive fictionalized biographies of popular composers, Heflin played friend, confidant, and inspiration to Jerome Kern (played by Robert Walker) in *Till the Clouds Roll By.* A few years later Heflin played Jennifer Jones's discarded husband in *Madame Bovary.* In *Possessed,* a turgid melodrama made in 1947, Heflin rejected Joan Crawford's love and paid for it dearly: she killed him.

Heflin also appeared in two of Hollywood's best Westerns, each time playing the second male lead. In *3:10 To Yuma* he was a farmer, hard up for money, who hired out to bring in gunman Glenn Ford. And in the more famous *Shane,* he

was Jean Arthur's pacifist husband who managed —but only just—to keep his family together despite the strong attraction between his wife and gunman Alan Ladd.

Back in the 1930s, Lew Ayers was well on his way to becoming established as a competent portrayer of brothers, friends, and other neutralized observers of romance. Ayers first gained acclaim as the young hero of *All Quiet on the Western Front,* an eloquent antiwar film made in 1930. Despite that good start, however, he was soon allowed to drift down to B pictures, then into secondary roles in bigger films.

Typical of these was *Rich Man, Poor Girl,* with

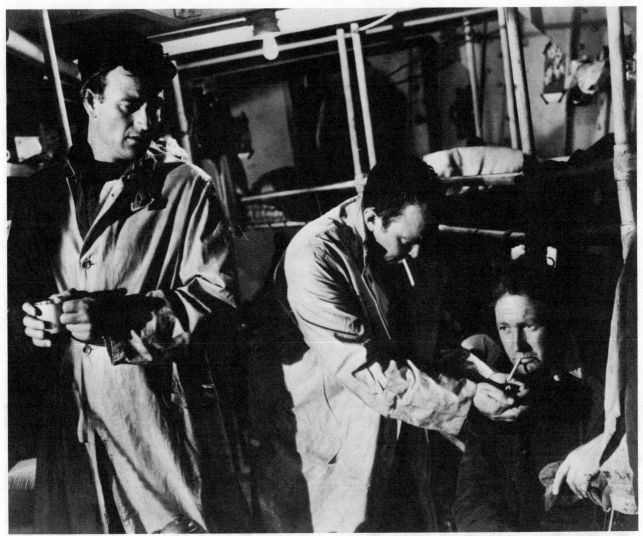

The Long Voyage Home. Based on Eugene O'Neill's play, this John Ford film had John Wayne as star, Thomas Mitchell as nice guy, and Ian Hunter as lost soul. (United Artists, 1940)

Robert Young and Ruth Hussey as the romantic leads. Ayers was the fiery young radical son of the poor family into which Young wanted to marry in this frothy comedy.

A better role was in *Holiday*, with Cary Grant and Katherine Hepburn. This time, Ayers was Miss Hepburn's hard-drinking, soft-spined brother who longs to escape a rich, domineering father but must settle for the satisfaction of seeing his rebellious sister (Hepburn) take Grant away from his snobbish sister (Doris Nolan).

There followed a few less rewarding parts. In *Ice Follies of 1939*, for instance, Ayers, Joan Crawford, and James Stewart all start out on ice skates. But before long, Ayers is forced to skate off into the wings while the camera follows the ups and downs of the Stewart-Crawford romance.

He was rescued (if that's the word) by the appearance of one James Kildare, a young intern who was destined to support Lew Ayers through a series of nine movies in the space of four years. In all of these, Ayers played the young assistant to Dr. Gillespie, the crusty old man portrayed by Lionel Barrymore. But late in 1942, the tenth film in the series was released, its title: *Dr. Gillespie's New Assistant*. Ayers had been replaced by Van Johnson.

Ironically, it was the First World War (or, at

H. M. Pulham, Esq. Van Heflin was Robert Young's close friend in this John P. Marquand story. Hedy Lamarr was the female star, although Young married Ruth Hussey. (MGM, 1941)

Till the Clouds Roll By. Robert Walker played composer Jerome Kern, and Van Heflin was his buddy in this song-studded semi-biography. (MGM, 1946)

The Feminine Touch. Rosalind Russell was only toying with Van Heflin here. The object: to make Ray Milland jealous. And, naturally, it worked. (MGM, 1941)

least a film about it) that helped launch Ayers's career; and it was the Second World War that virtually destroyed it. Called up for service, he declared himself a conscientious objector and brought down upon him the wrath of public and press. He performed noncombatant work during the war, then returned to resume his shattered career. His most important role after the war was in *Johnny Belinda,* opposite Jane Wyman.

This subcategory of Nice Friend/Brother brings to mind Barry Sullivan, who really fits better in the rival classification. However, one of his films belongs here and merits attention, not because it was a particularly good movie (it wasn't), but because it illustrates the flimsiness with which these supporting roles were sometimes drawn.

The movie in question was a 1950 pastiche titled *Grounds for Marriage,* an MGM entry starring Van Johnson and Kathryn Grayson. Johnson plays a throat doctor who doubles on oboe (that's right) in a "doctors' symphony." His ex-wife, Miss Grayson, is an opera singer who returns from an international tour, still in love with Johnson, who is now engaged to Paula Raymond. She wants to reunite with him, but he tells her: "You proved that opera and operations don't mix."

Sullivan is Johnson's brother, a toy manufacturer-playboy who has a yen for Kathryn. When Kathryn loses her voice (literally) after a stren-

uous performance, her trouble is diagnosed as emotional and it is suggested that "a new interest" might help her get over Van and also bring back her voice. (Johnson's training as Dr. Gillespie's new assistant apparently didn't do much good: in this film he mistakenly diagnoses his ex-wife's throat ailment as a rare tropical disease.) Sullivan begins courting Kathryn, who is now deprived of speech and reduced to scribbling notes, but he can't get anyplace. In the end she regains both her voice and her ex-husband, and brother Sullivan gets lost in the shuffle.

(Sullivan had an equally unrewarding role in the film version of *Lady in the Dark,* with Ginger Rogers and Ray Milland, playing Ginger's doctor.)

For an all-time, long-suffering Nice Friend, it would be difficult to match the record of Ian Hunter, an actor so firmly identified in the public's mind with losing that his name in the cast of any movie virtually robbed it of even the

Rich Man, Poor Girl. The title refers to Robert Young and Ruth Hussey, above. The other chap is Lew Ayers, who really didn't figure in the romance. (MGM, 1938)

Holiday. Binnie Barnes, Henry Daniell, Edward Everett Horton, Jean Dixon, Cary Grant, Katherine Hepburn, and Lew Ayers make up the tableau in this scene from a splendid film in which Ayers was a nice, if tipsy, friend. (Columbia, 1938)

Ice Follies of 1939. James Stewart, Lew Ayers, and Joan Crawford start out as an act, but in time Ayers is put on ice and Stewart and Crawford go on romancing. (MGM, 1939)

Grounds for Marriage. Kathryn Grayson, Van Johnson, Paula Raymond, and Barry Sullivan. Barry played Van's brother who made a half-hearted attempt to win Kathryn from him. (MGM, 1950)

Another Dawn. For Ian Hunter it was another graceful retreat. It was Errol Flynn who saw the sunrise with Kay Francis. (Warner Brothers, 1937)

slightest doubt as to the outcome of the story.

An indication of the kind of nobility Hunter was expected to portray was *Another Dawn*, a 1937 tear-jerker starring Errol Flynn and Kay Francis. Flynn plays a British officer stationed at some Sahara outpost. He falls in love with the wife (Miss Francis) of his commanding officer, Ian Hunter. Although Hunter loves his wife, he is so understanding and sympathetic that he finally flies off on a suicide mission, leaving Kay and Errol to each other. That's a Nice Friend.

In *That Certain Woman*, made the same year, Bette Davis works for attorney Ian Hunter, who loves her but is married. Bette marries Henry Fonda, but his rich father breaks up the marriage, even though Bette is pregnant. Bette and baby are both helped by Ian, who eventually dies, if only so that Bette and Fonda can be reunited.

He was Nice Friend in *Bittersweet*, with Jeanette MacDonald and Nelson Eddy. He lost Kay Francis (again) to George Brent in *Secrets of an Actress*. He was a doomed, aristocratic outcast in *The Long Voyage Home*.

Perhaps the classic Ian Hunter role was in a 1936 drama titled *To Mary with Love*. Myrna Loy was Mary and Warner Baxter was her imperfect husband. The story chronicled their

To Mary with Love. Nobody ever had a better friend than Ian Hunter. This time, he devoted his life to saving the marriage of Warner Baxter and Myrna Loy. (20th Century-Fox, 1936)

stormy marriage, through all of which Hunter stood on the sidelines, good friend to both, amateur marriage counselor when necessary and, of course, sticking rigidly to the rule that while we, the audience, might know of his secret love for her, Myrna—or Mary—never learns of it.

Hunter had a strong, if odd, role in *Strange*

Broadway Serenade. Stage-door Johnny was the role assigned Ian Hunter this time, but Jeanette MacDonald sang her songs to Lew Ayers. (MGM, 1939)

Strange Cargo. Joan Crawford and Clark Gable were the stars, and Ian Hunter was the mystical Nice Friend of all concerned. (MGM, 1940)

Cargo, a 1940 drama with Clark Gable and Joan Crawford. This concerns a group of escapees from a French penal colony, led by Gable and including Paul Lukas, Peter Lorre, Albert Dekker, and Hunter. Their bid for freedom is full of adventures and all of the men eventually come under the influence of the Christ-like Cambreau, played by Hunter. A past master at turning other cheeks, he exerts a spiritual sway over the criminals and in time even succeeds in reforming Gable, who almost kills him.

When he wasn't playing Nice Friend or God-figure, Hunter was still up to his jowls in loyalty.

He stood by Spencer Tracy through that star's vicissitudes as *Dr. Jekyll and Mr. Hyde*, and was a nice friendly doctor in *Edward, My Son*, with Tracy and Deborah Kerr.

Even when he played affluent producers, publishers, bankers, or tycoons—ready to ply heroines with diamond bracelets and the vision of a secure, serene life (offers almost invariably rejected, of course)—he did so with gentlemanly style and a kind of pathetic foreboding that he didn't stand a chance. He was a kind of Hollywood equivalent of Adlai Stevenson, of whom it was once said that the American people would

Shopworn Angel. Margaret Sullavan and James Stewart were in love, which left Walter Pidgeon little to do but wish them luck. (MGM, 1938)

Girl of the Golden West. Walter Pidgeon would have needed more than that gun to come between Nelson Eddy and Jeanette MacDonald. (MGM, 1938)

give him anything—except the presidency.

For a time, it looked as if Walter Pidgeon, who made many of his films at MGM, as did Hunter, was moving into the Hunter slot. He seemed to be on hand to complicate the romances of Clark Gable and Myrna Loy (in *Too Hot To Handle*) or MacDonald and Eddy (in *Girl of the Golden West*) or Myrna Loy and Franchot Tone (in *Manproof*) or Margaret Sullavan and James Stewart (in *The Shopworn Angel*).

But his career took an upturn with *Blossoms in the Dust*, in which he was teamed with Greer Garson. The success of this launched a box-office partnership that lasted through *Mrs. Miniver*, *Madame Curie*, *Mrs. Parkington*, *Julia Misbehaves*, and the inescapable attempt to recycle an earlier success, *The Miniver Story*.

In a lighter vein, and a later era, David Wayne did his bit to perpetuate the Nice Friend role. After effective appearances in *Adam's Rib*, with Tracy and Hepburn, and *A Portrait of Jennie*, with Jennifer Jones and Joseph Cotten, Wayne turned up in one of those 20th Century-Fox musicals, *My Blue Heaven*, with Betty Grable and Dan Dailey, which was long on songs and short on story.

One of his typical Nice Friend roles was in *The Reformer and the Redhead*, in which Dick Powell and June Allyson played the title roles.

Wayne was the loyal buddy of budding politician Powell in this light comedy. He had a similar (though better) part in *The Tender Trap*, with Frank Sinatra and Debbie Reynolds.

Perhaps because of his success in musicals on Broadway (he had been the original leprechaun in *Finian's Rainbow*) Wayne kept turning up in Hollywood musicals—*Wait Till the Sun Shines, Nellie, The I Don't Care Girl, Down Among the Sheltering Palms, With a Song in My Heart,* etc. —and gradually shifted from Nice Friend to leading man, but with only moderate success.

Despite the impressive record of suffering compiled by Ian Hunter, there was yet another natural born loser in films. He was Herbert Marshall, and although his long and successful career also included a good many leading roles, he somehow stays in the memory as a perennial also-ran, a Nice Friend/Likable Rival doomed to failure.

It was Mr. Marshall's ill fortune in films to be cuckolded again and again. While he stood by, all British dignity and well-bred silent suffering, a succession of his movie wives dallied with more dazzling partners. In *The Painted Veil*, Greta Garbo had a fling with George Brent. In *Angel*, Marlene Dietrich two-timed Marshall with Melvyn Douglas. Ever the gentleman, Marshall merely looked hurt and limped away into the back-

Dream Wife. Cary Grant seems left out as Walter Pidgeon huddles with Deborah Kerr. But don't you believe it: Pidgeon stepped aside again. (MGM, 1962)

The Reformer and the Redhead. That was Dick Powell and June Allyson. David Wayne was along mostly to keep warning Powell not to get involved with her. (MGM, 1950)

ground. (The limp was real, the result of a First World War injury.)

In *Riptide,* he was the jealous husband of Norma Shearer, his jealousy driving her into the waiting arms of Robert Montgomery. In *When Ladies Meet,* he was married to Joan Crawford, but Robert Taylor wound up with her. *Zaza* was different only in that it gave Marshall a chance to lose without a human rival: he loved Claudette Colbert but lost her to her career.

He was even more docile than usual in *The Letter,* a Somerset Maugham story in which his

wife (Bette Davis) not only has a lover but kills said lover and then turns to her trusting husband for solace. Marshall even spends his life's savings to buy the letter that proves his wife's infidelity —and then burns it and forgives her. (As a murderess, Miss Davis had to be punished in the film, even though Maugham's original ending had her getting away with her crime as well as her infidelity.)

But perhaps Marshall's greatest losing performance was in *The Dark Angel,* with Fredric March and Merle Oberon. In this one, Marshall

The Tender Trap. Friend David Wayne drank to Frank Sinatra's impending wedding (to Debbie Reynolds). In the next scene they both had monumental hangovers. (MGM, 1955)

When Ladies Meet. Beaten before he starts, Herbert Marshall is clearly no match for Robert Taylor. It was Taylor who wound up with Joan Crawford. (MGM, 1941)

Riptide. Husband Herbert Marshall drove Norma Shearer into the arms of Robert Montgomery this time. (MGM, 1934)

The Letter. Faithless Bette Davis two-timed husband Herbert Marshall, killed her lover, and was finally killed by another woman. (Warner Brothers, 1940)

The Little Foxes. Bette Davis neatly did away with invalid husband Herbert Marshall: she just cut off his medicine. (RKO, 1941)

marries Merle after her true love (March) is believed killed in the First World War. But soon March turns up, alive but blinded, and puts on an elaborate charade to hide his blindness (memorizing the location of objects in his home prior to a visit by Merle and Marshall) and avoid arousing their pity. But they see through his valiant gesture. In the end it is apparent that Marshall can't even win against a blind man: Merle goes to March.

At times, Marshall played a legitimate Nice Friend, as in *The Enchanted Cottage*, with Robert Young and Dorothy McGuire. In *The Little Foxes*, he was Bette Davis's invalid husband who is allowed to die (she merely withholds his medicine) because he opposes her avaricious schemes. But whether he was a friend, a cuckolded husband or a long-suffering suitor, Marshall was always so gentlemanly, so civilized, so lacking in personal magnetism that one could hardly regard him as a serious rival.

Before leaving this category, a few more actors deserve mention: Edmond O'Brien, who played heroes and villains, but somehow seemed most ef-

A Double Life. Schizophrenic actor Ronald Colman turned on his friend, Edmond O'Brien, eventually tried to kill his wife, while playing Othello. (Universal, 1948)

The Barefoot Contessa. Edmond O'Brien was a loud but likable press agent in this Joseph L. Mankiewicz drama. Ava Gardner and Humphrey Bogart were the stars. (United Artists, 1951)

fective as a Friend—in *A Double Life,* with Ronald Colman, and in *The Barefoot Contessa,* with Humphrey Bogart and Ava Gardner; Joseph Cotten's monumental friendship to Orson Welles in *Citizen Kane;* and Walter Abel, who was friend (both nice and funny), counselor, kindly parent, and even occasionally mock rival in a lifetime of movie making.

The Affairs of Susan. Walter Abel, right, was a familiar Nice Friend. The Susan of the title was Joan Fontaine, and her swains included Don DeFore (above), Dennis O'Keefe, and George Brent. (Paramount, 1945)

Citizen Kane. Charles Foster Kane (Orson Welles) had a true friend in Joseph Cotten—and another in Everett Sloane—as he planned his newspaper. (RKO, 1941)

4
The Rival

There is hardly a Hollywood producer, director, promotor, or agent who doesn't have a theory or two about what it is that constitutes that elusive commodity often described as a "star quality."

To braid all these theories into one master-theory is surely impossible. Merely to list some of the salient features of the more prevalent theories might be of some help.

The film star must have a strong, distinctive personality, reasonably good looks, a winning smile, an appeal to women without an offsetting offensiveness to men, a tolerable speaking voice, enough intelligence to be able to get some sense out of his lines—but preferably not so much that he dominates the director—an ability to look at ease in costume, some sort of grace of movement before the cameras, a shrewd grasp of what's "right" for him in selecting roles (assuming he has won that privilege), and, possibly most important, the knack for fitting into the shape of a screen character without entirely losing his own identity.

How all or even most of those traits could be said to fit such diverse stars as, say, Gary Cooper and Cary Grant, Spencer Tracy and John Wayne, Clark Gable and Bing Crosby, or James Stewart and Humphrey Bogart, may be hard to fathom. Yet all these men became stars by possessing to some degree or other most of those qualities. It

is, anyone must agree, no mean achievement.

Well, then, what of the Other Man? What special qualities does he need to become a successful Rival to the star? Are they different, or are they the very same qualities possessed to a lesser degree? And, if they are the same, would that guarantee that the successful Other Man will inevitably move up to star status?

There have, of course, been many Other Men who later became stars in their own right—Robert Young, David Niven, Melvyn Douglas, Don Ameche, and Ray Milland, to name only a few. But during the time that they were Other Men—and were accepted by the public as such—the chemistry had to be somehow different. Discarding Ralph Bellamy roles, Funny Friends, and Nice Friends, all of whom were clearly labeled as not being serious competitors for the heroine's hand or any other part of her anatomy, let's see what special qualities the Rival needed.

He might or might not be better looking than the star. He must have a strong (though not necessarily likable) personality. He must be attractive to women (not only to the leading lady but to those women in the audience who would identify with her) and yet not quite so attractive that when he is finally rejected the feminine star will seem to have made a stupid choice.

In short, he must suggest a valid alternative

for the heroine—and yet somehow fall just shy of the mark, so that the ending is "satisfying" to the audience.

(Once again, it is not the intention here to dismiss the contributions of the writer, who must create the character and plot, the producer who must cast the part, and the director who must draw a successful performance from the actor. Recognizing all of that, however, it is still upon the actor's shoulders that blame for failure or praise for success will rest.)

Given that background, it should be evident that those actors who succeeded in establishing themselves as acceptable Rivals—whether or not they later moved up to stardom—have earned the respect and admiration of any movie fan. The gallery of Rivals that follows serves to support that view.

One of the most inveterate of film actors in any category has been David Niven. His remarkable career in films began in the mid-1930s and was still in high gear three decades later. Some of his best work was done in Other Men roles, ranging anywhere from Nice Friend to viable Rival.

Niven didn't start at the top. His stormy youth had included sporadic attendance at several schools, a stint in the British Army, some elbow-rubbing with glamorous people—but virtually no theatrical training. In Hollywood, he did extra work first, then began getting a few speaking parts. In 1935, he was a Cockney sailor in *Barbary Coast,* a year later he played an inconsequential Englishman in *Dodsworth,* and an English major in *Beloved Enemy,* which had Brian Aherne and Merle Oberon in the starring roles. He was a stiff-upper-lipped British officer again in *The Charge of the Light Brigade,* starring Errol Flynn.

His first good Rival part came in *Bluebeard's Eighth Wife,* in which he represented a debonair alternative to Gary Cooper for the love of Claudette Colbert.

Next came good supporting roles in *The Prisoner of Zenda,* with Ronald Colman and Madeleine Carroll, and *Dawn Patrol,* with Errol Flynn again. He did justice to the exacting Other Man role of Edgar in *Wuthering Heights,* with Laurence Olivier and Merle Oberon, and played an unscrupulous Aaron Burr in *The Magnificent Doll,* with Ginger Rogers. Soon he was playing

leading roles—opposite Loretta Young in *Eternally Yours,* Ginger Rogers in *Bachelor Mother,* and Olivia de Havilland in *Raffles.*

Even when he passed the peak of his appeal as a leading man, Niven was by no means finished. He was still a delightful Rival in *The Moon Is Blue,* in which he lost Maggie McNamara to William Holden; in *The Little Hut,* in which he vied with Stewart Granger for Ava Gardner; and in lesser items like *The Toast of New Orleans,* in which he loved Kathryn Grayson, who chose Mario Lanza.

Niven, in the mid-1950s, starred in one of the biggest hits of that decade, *Around the World in Eighty Days,* and two years later, at long last, he was awarded an Oscar for his performance in *Separate Tables.*

A case might be made for the peculiar suitability of British actors to play Other Men roles —and more particularly Rivals—in American films.

There have, of course, been many British stars in Hollywood films, from the 1930s on. One thinks of Ronald Colman, Errol Flynn, Leslie Howard, Charles Laughton, Herbert Marshall, Laurence Olivier, and Robert Donat, among others.

But as against that, there were many Britishers who built their careers on Other Men roles—Ian

Bluebeard's Eighth Wife. Claudette Colbert was spouse number eight to Gary Cooper, and David Niven (above) was a poor second. (Paramount, 1938)

The Moon Is Blue. When all the giggling was over, Maggie McNamara chose William Holden over David Niven in this mildly risqué comedy. (United Artists, 1953)

The Magnificent Doll. Ginger Rogers played Dolly Madison and David Niven played Aaron Burr, one of the bigger losers of American history. (Universal, 1946)

Hunter, George Sanders, Basil Rathbone, Alan Marshall, Peter Lawford, Michael Rennie, Michael Wilding, and, for a time, Niven (plus such British Funny Friends and Nice Friends as Reginald Gardiner, Reginald Denny, Nigel Bruce, Alan Mowbray, and Roland Young).

It could be that some subliminal chauvinistic feeling, some residue of resentment by former "colonials" against former "imperialists," some secret satisfaction in seeing a regular, down-to-earth American leading man win out over a slick, sophisticated Englishman—it could be that these things made movie fans respond favorably to seeing British actors in Rival roles pitted against homegrown heroes. Perhaps, too, there was something else involved: a British actor was often better qualified to play urbane, articulate, poetry-spouting lovesick suitors who were bound to lose to rugged, iconoclastic American men of action.

But the theory can be carried only so far, since there have also been many cases of Britishers losing to other Britishers and, more rarely, of Britishers winning over Americans. In any case, British actors do tend to make good Rivals, as some of the ensuing evidence will indicate.

The mild-mannered, gentlemanly Brian Aherne lost Katherine Hepburn to Cary Grant in *Sylvia Scarlet* (1935) and Claudette Colbert to Ray Milland in *Skylark*. In *Juarez*, he was the luckless Maximillian, for whose life Carlotta (Bette Davis)

Juarez. Bette Davis was the Empress Carlotta, Brian Aherne was the hapless Maximilian in this drama about Mexico's struggle for independence. The officer at left is Gilbert Roland. (Warner Brothers, 1939)

Sylvia Scarlett. Brian Aherne looks doubtful, Cary Grant smug, as Katherine Hepburn tangles with Edmund Gwenn. Grant won the girl, of course. (RKO, 1935)

pleaded in vain. Even as recently as 1963, he was King Arthur, losing Jean Wallace to Cornel Wilde in *Lancelot and Guinivere.*

Basil Rathbone had a long and richly varied career, which included some memorable Rivals. He duelled (and lost to) Errol Flynn in *Captain Blood* and *The Adventures of Robin Hood,* had the same experience with Tyrone Power in *The Mark of Zorro,* was a Gestapo chief in *Above Suspicion,* with Joan Crawford and Fred MacMurray, the foe of Gary Cooper in *The Adventures of Marco Polo,* and an unmitigated cad in *Confession,* with Kay Francis. He was rebuffed by Joan Fontaine in *Frenchman's Creek,* played

a Nazi again in *Paris Calling,* and an evil Richard II in *Tower of London.*

Later, Rathbone became the personification of Sherlock Holmes in a dozen films about the famed Baker Street sleuth, with Nigel Bruce ever on hand in the classic Nice Friend role of Dr. Watson.

Equally as villainous as Rathbone, and conveying the same sort of snobbish superiority that audiences liked to see shot down was George Sanders.

He first attracted American audiences as Madeleine Carroll's unsavory husband in *Lloyds of London,* which starred Tyrone Power. He was a mean Nazi in *Confessions of a Nazi Spy* and a World War One Prussian heavy in *Nurse Edith Cavell*. He tried to come between Jeanette MacDonald and Nelson Eddy (what a hope!) in *Bittersweet*, failed to win Norma Shearer away from Robert Taylor in *Her Cardboard Lover*, and opposed Tyrone Power twice more, in *Son of Fury* and *The Black Swan*.

Sanders lived a sort of double screen life. Sandwiched in between these various villainies, he appeared as both *The Saint* and *The Falcon* in several B pictures in which he played these amateur sleuths fighting crime. (Later, Sanders's real-life brother, Tom Conway, took over the *Falcon* series.)

One of Sanders's most successful roles, for which he won a Best Supporting Actor Oscar, was as the conniving theater critic and gossip columnist in *All About Eve*.

When Alan Marshall first began appearing in Hollywood films, in 1936, he must have seemed to some a potential successor to Ronald Colman. His early pictures included *The Garden of Allah*, with Charles Boyer and Marlene Dietrich, and *Conquest*, with Boyer and Garbo.

He was a cad in *Parnell*, with Clark Gable and

Skylark. Wife Claudette Colbert had a minor fling with Brian Aherne, but came to her senses and returned to husband Ray Milland. (Paramount, 1941)

Lancelot and Guinevere. Brian Aherne (seated) was poor King Arthur, listening to all the chatter while Guinivere (Jean Wallace) was in beautiful downtown Camelot with Lancelot (Cornel Wilde). (Universal, 1936)

Above Suspicion. Joan Crawford and Fred MacMurray were the stars, and Basil Rathbone turned out to be the bad guy. Surprise! (MGM, 1943)

The Adventures of Robin Hood. Claude Rains and Olivia de Havilland listen while Basil Rathbone denounces Errol Flynn. It didn't help—Flynn won Olivia. (Warner Brothers, 1938)

Crossroads. William Powell doesn't look too worried over being tied up by Basil Rathbone. In the end it was Powell, of course, who got Hedy Lamarr. (MGM, 1942)

Bitter Sweet. Whatever sinister looks passed between Ian Hunter and George Sanders, at the end Jeanette MacDonald was still true to Nelson Eddy. (MGM, 1940)

Her Cardboard Lover. Norma Shearer had little difficulty in choosing between George Sanders and Robert Taylor. (MGM, 1942)

Assignment: Paris. George Sanders was the editor, Marta Toren was the glamorous spy, and Audrey Totter made wisecracks. Dana Andrews was the crusading reporter. (Columbia, 1952)

All About Eve. All listening to Gregory Ratoff are Anne Baxter, Marilyn Monroe, Gary Merrill, George Sanders, and Celeste Holm. This splendid Joseph L. Mankiewicz film gave Sanders one of his best roles, plus an Oscar. (20th Century-Fox, 1950)

Myrna Loy, and Irene Dunne's tragic husband in *The White Cliffs of Dover*. He was a Rival in *He Stayed for Breakfast*, with Loretta Young and Melvyn Douglas, a loser again in *I Met My Love Again*, with Henry Fonda and Joan Bennett, and once more in *Irene*, with Ray Milland and Anna Neagle. Somehow, he never quite made the step up to leading man in major pictures.

By 1949, after a series of B pictures, he was reduced to membership in that hopeless army of men who have, at one time or another, turned up in Fred Astaire-Ginger Rogers musicals, pretend-ing to be Rival suitors in what was clearly an impossible situation. (Fred and Ginger were as predictably inseparable as Ma and Pa Kettle.)

Peter Lawford fared somewhat better. True, he had the thankless task of playing an Astaire rival of sorts in *Easter Parade*, but he supported Frank Sinatra and Kathryn Grayson in *It Happened in Brooklyn*, and Jennifer Jones and Charles Boyer in *Cluny Brown*. He was a definite Rival in *You For Me*, losing Jane Greer to Gig Young. He had no chance against Jack Lemmon in *It Should Happen to You*, with Judy Holiday. Having

Parnell. Edna Mae Oliver stands by while Myrna Loy has a scene with husband Alan Marshall in this botched drama about Irish politics. Clark Gable was Parnell. (MGM, 1937)

He Stayed for Breakfast. Loretta Young and Una O'Connor flank Alan Marshall. But Melvyn Douglas outflanked him. (Columbia, 1940)

played his share of Rivals, he was elevated to leading roles opposite June Allyson, Esther Williams, and the like, and to heavier (if not always rewarding) dramatic roles in *Exodus, Sylvia, Harlow, Oceans Eleven,* and *Advise and Consent.*

A chronic loser in films was Michael Wilding, whose self-effacing manner and simpering demeanor almost doomed him to such roles. Imported from Britain after making a number of films with Anna Neagle, Wilding didn't make the ocean voyage as successfully as some of his compatriots.

He worked twice for Alfred Hitchcock, both times in 1950. In *Stage Fright*, he was outdis-

tanced by Jane Wyman, Marlene Dietrich, and Richard Todd. In *Under Capricorn*, with Ingrid Bergman and Joseph Cotten, he was friend to Bergman, whose marriage to the moody Cotten seemed constantly threatened. But in the end, Cotten and Bergman were reconciled and Wilding exited gracefully but empty-armed.

Wilding had another secondary role in *The Egyptian*, which starred Edmund Purdom and emerged a boring flop. But he was starred opposite Leslie Caron in *The Glass Slipper*, in a Prince Charming role better suited to his ephemeral talents. He stood by pointlessly while William Holden fell in love with Nancy Kwan in *The World*

It Happened in Brooklyn. Jimmy Durante, Frank Sinatra, Peter Lawford, and Kathryn Grayson. No Englishman could win on Sinatra's home turf. (MGM, 1947)

Under Capricorn. Despite his love for Ingrid Bergman, Michael Wilding declined to bust up her shaky marriage to Joseph Cotten. (Warner Brothers, 1949)

of *Suzie Wong*, and again in *A Girl Named Tamiko*, which involved Laurence Harvey and France Nuyen. And Wilding was also in *The Naked Edge*, which was Gary Cooper's last—and far from his best—film.

Like so many other English actors, Michael Rennie had some respectable credits behind him when he first switched to American films. His first good American role was in the excellent spy drama *Five Fingers*, which starred James Mason.

But then Rennie was trapped in two rather inferior remakes. He played the leading role of Jean Valjean in *Les Miserables*, but he didn't match Fredric March's earlier version of the part and the picture on the whole didn't measure up to its distinguished predecessor. Rennie also appeared in *The Rains of Ranchipur*, a rehash of *The Rains Came*, with Lana Turner and Richard Burton in the roles originally done by Myrna Loy and Tyrone Power. Rennie had the unhappy role

Easter Parade. Peter Lawford, Ann Miller, and Fred Astaire. Missing is Judy Garland, who starred opposite Astaire. (MGM, 1948)

The Scarlet Coat. Michael Wilding played an aide to Benedict Arnold in this costume drama. The inevitable winner was Cornel Wilde. (MGM, 1955)

The Loves of Omar Khayyam. Michael Rennie might well be contemplating suicide. Once again, he lost to Cornel Wilde. (Paramount, 1956)

of the husband, first played by George Brent.

He was lost amid a welter of names in *Island in the Sun* (James Mason, Harry Belafonte, Joan Fontaine) and subordinated to Cornel Wilde and Raymond Massey in *Omar Khayyam*. But Rennie bounced back nicely in a legitimate Rival role in the comedy *Mary, Mary,* supporting Debbie Reynolds and Barry Nelson.

In between, Rennie fell victim to that peculiar Hollywood belief that English actors have the sort of impeccable diction that makes them ideal for historical and/or biblical epics in which togas and sandals are worn. He was in *The Robe, Demetrius and the Gladiator,* and *Princess of the Nile.*

Before leaving the British-born actors who have labored in Hollywood's rivalry vineyards, one more demands attention, even though he became such a Hollywood fixture that a whole generation of moviegoers may not even recall that he was, in fact, English-born and not American.

This was Ray Milland, who was destined to become a top leading man in dozens of Hollywood films, but who, like so many others, served his time in Rival parts first.

Milland was in Hollywood by the early 1930s, was killed by Charles Laughton in *Payment Deferred,* in 1932; played a gigolo in *Bolero,* with George Raft and Carole Lombard; and had a secondary part in *The Glass Key,* again with Raft.

Then came some good Other Men roles: in *The Gilded Lily,* he rivalled Fred MacMurray for Claudette Colbert and lost. He also lost Margaret Sullavan to James Stewart in *Next Time We Love.* He was almost totally lost in *Three Smart Girls,* a Deanna Durbin vehicle, and in *Many Happy Returns,* a Burns and Allen comedy.

Milland fared better in *Men With Wings,* again with Fred MacMurray, in *Beau Geste,* with Gary Cooper and Robert Preston, and in *I Wanted Wings,* with William Holden and Veronica Lake. But love interest in these action films was secondary.

Reap the Wild Wind had one of those tidy quartet casts: Milland and John Wayne, Paulette Goddard and Susan Hayward. In *Everything Happens at Night,* Milland and Robert Cummings were both after Sonja Henie.

By the mid-1940s, Milland was playing romantic leads: *Skylark* and *Arise My Love,* both with Claudette Colbert; *The Lady Has Plans* and *The*

Mary, Mary. Barry Nelson confronts Michael Rennie, knowing full well that Debbie Reynolds is his for keeps. (Warner Brothers, 1963)

Next Time We Love. Ray Milland stands by while James Stewart and Margaret Sullavan bill and coo. Milland did a lot of standing by in those days. (Universal, 1936)

Crystal Ball, both with Paulette Goddard; and *The Major and the Minor* and *Lady in the Dark,* both with Ginger Rogers.

In 1945, Milland won an Academy Award for his impressive work in *The Lost Weekend,* and then had a tough time topping that movie. (He was concerned with alcoholism again in *Night into Morning,* with John Hodiak; and in *Something To Live For* his wife, Joan Fontaine, was an alcoholic.)

Milland's career as a star lasted for a long time, but it's worth noting that the studios for which he worked kept tossing him into the strangest films. He had little to do but stare at Dorothy Lamour's sarong in *Jungle Princess, Her Jungle Love,* and once more in *Tropic Holiday.* He had to masquerade as a gypsy for *Golden Earrings,* with Marlene Dietrich. And the combination of Milland and Hedy Lamarr resulted in a stultifying western called *Copper Canyon.* In *The Girl in the Red Velvet Swing,* he was killed by Farley Granger.

Of the many American-born full-fledged Rivals, several went on to stardom while others moved to character roles. Among the more successful were Robert Cummings, Melvyn Douglas, Franchot Tone, George Brent, Robert Montgomery, and Robert Young.

Cummings, whose brash charm and flair for comedy served him well for many years both in feature films and later in television, did a number of secondary roles before moving up to leads.

As early as the mid-1930s, he was turning up in such big films as *So Red the Rose*, with Margaret Sullavan and Randolph Scott; *Souls At Sea*, with Gary Cooper and Frances Dee; *Wells Fargo*, with Joel McCrea; and *The Texans*, with Randolph Scott.

His boyish smile made him effective in such Deanna Durbin films as *Three Smart Girls Grow Up*, *Spring Parade*, and *It Started with Eve*.

He lost Betty Grable to Don Ameche in *Moon Over Miami*. He was excess baggage in *You and Me*, which was concerned with George Raft and Sylvia Sidney, the same in *Last Train from Madrid*, with Lew Ayers and Dorothy Lamour.

But Cummings was most impressive in *The Devil and Miss Jones*, with Jean Arthur and Charles Coburn. This was a 1941 comedy in which Coburn played a department store tycoon who took a job in his own store (incognito, of course) to root out union agitators, and Cummings, besides being Miss Arthur's beau, was the leading agitator.

The Gilded Lily. Ray Milland puts on a brave smile as Fred MacMurray and Claudette Colbert kiss, but as usual it was Fred who won. (Paramount, 1935)

The Girl in the Red Velvet Swing. Ray Milland played famed architect Stanford White in this turn-of-the-century drama. He dallied with Joan Collins, wife of Farley Granger, and paid with his life. (20th Century-Fox, 1955)

Spring Parade. Robert Cummings was again in quest of Deanna Durbin, and again he didn't make it. (Universal, 1940)

It Started with Eve. Robert Cummings was involved with Deanna Durbin in this comedy. The ladies above are Catherine Doucet and Margaret Tallichet. (Universal, 1941)

Moon over Miami. That air of confidence about Robert Cummings meant nothing. It was Don Ameche who walked off with Betty Grable. (20th Century-Fox, 1941)

Everything Happens at Night. Robert Cummings (above) and Ray Milland were rival reporters in pursuit of Sonja Henie. (20th Century-Fox, 1939)

Once he'd hit his stride—in that comedy and in a serious dramatic role in *King's Row* the following year, Cummings went on and on, making one light comedy after another. When television came along, he was one of the first Hollywood stars to make the transition successfully and starred in his own program for several years.

Melvyn Douglas was another top-ranking actor who was adept at playing either tempting Rivals or girl-winning heroes. He arrived in Hollywood (from the stage) in 1930, appearing in a succession of undistinguished films until 1936, when he was in *The Gorgeous Hussy*, starring Joan Crawford. In this costume drama, Douglas rejected Crawford, who then married first Robert Taylor and then Franchot Tone.

But in the same year, Douglas made *Theodora Goes Wild*, opposite Irene Dunne, and demonstrated a flair for light comedy that was to boost

The Gorgeous Hussy. Joan Crawford listens to Melvyn Douglas. Her first husband (Robert Taylor) was already killed and later she turned to Franchot Tone. Douglas just turned grey. (MGM, 1936)

his career. Among the films that followed were *Angel,* with Marlene Dietrich, and the brilliant *Ninotchka,* with Garbo.

Although he was now playing leading men, he appeared again as a Rival in *Too Many Husbands,* with Jean Arthur and Fred MacMurray—that old standby about the first husband being thought dead, only to turn up just as the "widow" is about to remarry. Then he switched back to hero again in *That Uncertain Feeling,* with Merle Oberon.

The Second World War took him away from films for several years, after which he played the Other Man role in *Sea of Grass,* with Spencer Tracy and Katherine Hepburn; a prop Rival in *Mr. Blandings Builds His Dream House,* with Cary Grant and Myrna Loy; a more serious Rival in *The Great Sinner,* with Gregory Peck and Ava Gardner; and a villain in *My Forbidden Past,* with Robert Mitchum and Ava Gardner.

When Douglas was already in his sixties, he won an Academy Award as Best Supporting Actor as Paul Newman's stern father in *Hud.*

Even after so many years, it's difficult for a movie fan to erase from his mind the image of Franchot Tone as it was projected in the 1930s. Tone, invariably in white tie and tails, a cocktail glass in one hand and a cigarette in the other, was the symbol of aristocratic decadence. If he wasn't tempting the heroine toward the primrose path he was trying to corrupt the poor-but-honest hero.

Witness *Dancing Lady,* an MGM picture that gave Tone one of his first big parts. Joan Crawford was the lady of the title, a poor girl determined to tap her way to stardom, and Clark Gable was the hard-boiled Broadway director looking for a hit. Tone, the dilettante playboy, first sees Joan in the pony line of a burlesque, secretly arranges to get her an audition with Gable, and later (still secretly) pumps money into the show Gable is rehearsing, to ensure Joan's job. She has already rebuffed Tone's improper advances, but he doesn't give up easily.

Joan falls for Gable and he, despite his gruffness, gradually recognizes that she isn't the playboy's plaything he originally suspected. In time, she is elevated to the starring role in the musical (the "star" having proved inadequate) and all looks rosy. We are even treated to a demonstra-

Too Many Husbands. Melvyn Douglas already has the look of the loser in this scene with Fred MacMurray and Jean Arthur. (Columbia, 1940)

Sea of Grass. Melvyn Douglas and Katherine Hepburn. But with Spencer Tracy in the cast, you know how much chance Douglas had. (MGM, 1947)

The Great Sinner. Not all of Melvyn Douglas's urbane manner could lure Ava Gardner away from Gregory Peck in this drama. (MGM, 1949)

tion of Joan's terpsichorean talents in a rehearsal scene in which she's partnered by Fred Astaire, who mysteriously turns up for this scene only.

But then Tone realizes that if Joan becomes a star she won't need him. So he sabotages the production—closing it just before the scheduled premiere—and invites the unsuspecting (and now unemployed) Joan for a cruise on his yacht. Only after she returns does she learn the truth. She then goes back into the show—which Gable is miraculously financing on his own—and all ends well, except Tone's scheme for winning Joan.

This was Franchot Tone in 1933—rich, attractive, corrupt, and doomed to losing the girl. It

launched a long and unwavering career as Rival.

In *No More Ladies* (1935) he lost Joan Crawford to Robert Taylor. The same year in *Reckless,* William Powell won Jean Harlow—and Tone committed suicide. In *Love on the Run* (1936) he lost Joan again to Gable. In *They Gave Him a Gun* he was Spencer Tracy's wartime buddy who turned into a vicious killer.

In the midst of his growing popularity, he made *The Lives of a Bengal Lancer,* with Gary Cooper, and *Mutiny on the Bounty,* with Clark Gable and Charles Laughton. He was good in both, but the star in neither.

Three Loves Has Nancy had Tone losing Janet

Gaynor to Robert Montgomery. And in *Three Comrades,* he lost Margaret Sullavan to Robert Taylor. In *True to Life,* Dick Powell beat him out for Mary Martin.

By now, Tone was edging past the young playboy age, so he was cast as an older playboy. In *Nice Girl?* he was too old for Deanna Durbin—but Robert Stack wasn't. In *Honeymoon* he naturally had to yield Shirley Temple to Guy Madison. (He made two more pictures with Durbin, *His Butler's Sister* and *Because of Him*—neither of which did much to enhance anybody's reputation.)

In 1948, he was back to playing the Other Man again, this time in *Every Girl Should Be Married,* with Cary Grant and Betsy Drake. He did play some leading roles in the intervening years, but his image as the wealthy spoiled son of the rich lingered on, long after he was able to exploit it effectively.

To some extent, Robert Montgomery's image was similar to Tone's, at least in his earlier films. Another playboy in evening clothes, Montgomery was just right in such pictures as *Forsaking All Others,* in which he watched Clark Gable sail away with Joan Crawford, *The Last of Mrs.*

Dancing Lady. Joan Crawford is amused at Franchot Tone's appearance, even if Richard Carle isn't. Playboy Tone couldn't compete with Clark Gable for Joan. (MGM, 1933)

Cheyney (this time it was William Powell taking Crawford away from Montgomery), *Riptide* (in which he dallied with Norma Shearer, who was married to Herbert Marshall), and *Night Flight*, again with Gable, but with Helen Hayes as the leading lady.

But Montgomery in time escaped the trap and went on to such distinguished films as *Night Must Fall, Yellow Jack, Here Comes Mr. Jordan,* and *They were Expendable.*

Another habitual loser was George Brent, of the expressionless face and the nasal voice. He was Garbo's lover in *The Painted Veil,* but she eventually returned to husband Herbert Marshall. In *Forty Second Street* he was a kept man, Bebe Daniels slipping him money for dinner under the restaurant table. In *Jezebel,* he was knocked off in a duel to make way for Henry Fonda, but Bette Davis eventually did Fonda dirt, too, losing everything but winning an Academy Award. Brent was jilted by Davis again in *In This Our Life,* but both she and Dennis Morgan ended up dead. In *The Rains Came,* he was married to Myrna Loy, who fell in love with Tyrone Power. In *Wings of the Navy,* he lost Olivia de Havilland to his younger brother, John Payne. And in

Love on the Run. Franchot Tone seems to have an edge on Clark Gable, but it can't last. Naturally, Gable won Joan Crawford again. (MGM, 1936)

Three Loves Has Nancy. Janet Gaynor was Nancy, Robert Montgomery was the winner, Franchot Tone the loser. (MGM, 1938)

Till We Meet Again, a remake of *One Way Passage,* he and Merle Oberon were both doomed to disaster.

But Brent played some leads, too, as in *Dark Victory,* with Bette Davis, *The Great Lie,* with Davis and Mary Astor, and a good many action B pictures in which he played crusading D.A.s, special agents, fearless detectives, and the like. In 1949, he was back to losing again in *Bride for Sale,* with Claudette Colbert and Robert Young.

Which brings us to one of the most persistent losers in movie history—and one of the most durable stars—Robert Young. It's doubtful if anyone can match his record of ill-fated movie roles.

Young began in movies as an extra, worked his way up. By 1931, when he was only twenty-four, he was getting featured roles. Then his string of Other Men roles began:

In 1932, he played a murderer in *Unashamed,* with Helen Twelvetrees.

In 1933, he supported Gary Cooper and Joan Crawford in *Today We Live.* Young died.

In 1934, he was one of Wellington's officers in *The House of Rothschild,* which starred George Arliss and Loretta Young.

In 1935, he began losing brides to a succession of stars in a series of unrelated films: in *The Bride Comes Home,* Claudette Colbert came home

Every Girl Should Be Married. The girl in question was Betsy Drake and she chose Cary Grant rather than Franchot Tone. (RKO, 1948)

The Saxon Charm. Robert Montgomery (seen here with John Payne) was a ruthless Broadway producer in this, one of his more serious and less successful films. (Universal, 1948)

to Fred MacMurray; in *The Bride Walks Out,* Barbara Stanwyck walked out on Young and back to Gene Raymond; in *The Bride Wore Red,* Young lost Joan Crawford to Franchot Tone.

In 1937, he lost Colbert again, this time to Melvyn Douglas in *I Met Him in Paris.*

In 1938, Young was shot in a duel in *The Toy Wife,* which starred Luise Rainer and Melvyn Douglas. The same year he lost Simone Simon to Don Ameche in *Josette.* He also lost Joan Crawford to Melvyn Douglas in *The Shining Hour.* And in *Three Comrades,* with Margaret Sullavan, Robert Taylor, and Franchot Tone, Young was the comrade who got killed. In 1940, he was engaged to Margaret Sullavan in *The Mortal Storm,*

but then he turned Nazi and she turned to James Stewart.

That same year, he was in a supporting role with Spencer Tracy in *Northwest Passage* and with Randolph Scott in *Western Union.* And to make Young's year perfect he was wrongly diagnosed by Lew Ayers in *Dr. Kildare's Crisis.*

Finally, in 1941, his big break came. MGM gave him the starring role in *H. M. Pulham, Esquire,* with Hedy Lamarr and Ruth Hussey. He did so well that other good pictures followed, including *Claudia,* the inevitable sequel, *Claudia and David, The Enchanted Cottage,* and many more.

Young also holds the distinction of being one

Jezebel. George Brent loved Bette Davis, who loved Henry Fonda, who married Margaret Lindsay. Brent was killed in a duel and Fonda got leprosy. (Warner Brothers, 1938)

Bride for Sale. This time out, George Brent lost Claudette Colbert to Robert Young. (RKO, 1949)

Forsaking All Others. Robert Montgomery (in early drag) had no hope of beating Clark Gable to Joan Crawford's side. (MGM, 1934)

The Last of Mrs. Cheyney. With veteran Funny Friend Nigel Bruce (later Dr. Watson to Basil Rathbone's Sherlock Holmes) is loser Robert Montgomery. He played a titled cad. (MGM, 1937)

of the very few stars to hit the jackpot twice in television. For years he starred in the successful comedy series, "Father Knows Best." Then, after a lengthy period of relative inactivity, he came back with the equally successful "Marcus Welby, M.D." (The only other star who has matched that has been Raymond Burr, with "Perry Mason," followed by "Ironside.")

Next to Young's record as an unsuccessful Rival, anyone else's pales. And yet there have been others who deserve some attention.

To begin with, there's Joseph Cotten, who went to Hollywood with Orson Welles's Mercury Theater and stayed. He was Welles's faithful friend in *Citizen Kane.* But he was a killer in Hitchcock's *Shadow of a Doubt* and again (much later) in *Niagara.* He fought Gregory Peck in *Duel in the Sun,* and lost Jennifer Jones to him. He was mean to his alcoholic brother (Van Johnson) in *Bottom of the Bottle* and turned to crime in *The Steel Trap.* Cotten fared better, however, in such films as *Gaslight, Portrait of Jennie,* and *Love Letters.*

Gene Raymond was a fairly consistent loser in

Slave Girl. It's only a temporary setback. This time, George Brent won the girl (Yvonne de Carlo) even though the film was a minor one. (Universal, 1947)

I Met Him in Paris. Robert Young was one of three suitors after Claudette Colbert. Winner was Melvyn Douglas, and Lee Bowman ran a poor third. (Paramount, 1937)

The Toy Wife. That was Luise Rainer, seen here with winner Melvyn Douglas and loser Robert Young. (MGM, 1938)

Three Comrades. They were Robert Taylor, Franchot Tone, and Robert Young, and the girl was Margaret Sullavan. Young was killed this time. (MGM, 1938)

some of his films. He lost Joan Crawford to Franchot Tone in *Sadie McKee*. He lost Carole Lombard to Robert Montgomery in *Mr. and Mrs. Smith*. And he lost Jeanette MacDonald to Brian Aherne in *Smilin' Through*.

John Howard lost Katherine Hepburn to Cary Grant in *The Philadelphia Story*. And in the remake, *High Society*, John Lund had the same role, losing Grace Kelly to Bing Crosby.

Zachary Scott, who started out as a dashing villain in *The Mask of Demetrios*, ran into trouble with Joan Crawford in two films: in *Mildred Pierce*, her daughter (Ann Blyth) killed Scott; in *Flamingo Road*, he killed himself. He was also a

losing Rival in *Those Endearing Young Charms*, with Robert Young and Laraine Day, and *Let's Make It Legal*, with Claudette Colbert and Macdonald Carey.

Carey himself did his share of losing. He was the other man in *Take a Letter Darling*, with Rosalind Russell and Fred MacMurray; and in *Suddenly It's Spring*, with MacMurray and Paulette Goddard.

Until he made the step up to leading roles, Dana Andrews did a lot of hanging about in the background of a number of films. He played the second lead in *A Wing and a Prayer*, supporting Don Ameche. He was a seriocomic gangster in

Duel in the Sun. The duellers were Gregory Peck and Joseph Cotten and the prize was Jennifer Jones. Peck won all. (United Artists, 1946)

Ball of Fire, with Gary Cooper and Barbara Stanwyck, and a soldier in *Up In Arms,* with Danny Kaye and Dinah Shore. In *Daisy Kenyon,* he was aced out by Henry Fonda, who won Joan Crawford.

Adolphe Menjou had a long and active career in a variety of Rival roles. One of his earliest successes (1930) was as the conniving editor in *The Front Page,* with Pat O'Brien as the reporter. Two years later he was both friend and Rival to Gary Cooper in *A Farewell to Arms,* with Helen Hayes as the damsel in the offing. Menjou was an engaging gambler in *Little Miss Marker,* which served to make little Shirley Temple a star. He romped through *Turnabout,* in which Carole Landis and John Hubbard switched clothes. He tried

to come between Fred Astaire and Rita Hayworth in *You Were Never Lovelier* and complicated the romance of Betty Grable and Robert Young in *Sweet Rosie O'Grady.*

As he grew older, Menjou took on more character roles, including a memorable one as a corrupt military officer in director Stanley Kubrick's first big success, *Paths of Glory.*

Before he learned that there was money (and more fun) in mock horror films, Vincent Price established a good reputation as a smooth and sinister Rival. He was Sir Walter Raleigh in *The Private Lives of Elizabeth and Essex,* which starred Bette Davis and Errol Flynn. He was as urbane and catty as Clifton Webb in *Laura,* but it didn't do either of them any good with Gene

Two Flags West. Jeff Chandler (back to camera) faces Joseph Cotten and Cornel Wilde. The lady in question was Linda Darnell. (20th Century-Fox, 1950)

Smilin' Through. Jealousy drives Gene Raymond to terrible deeds in this famous tear-jerker. The inseparable lovers were Jeanette MacDonald and Brian Aherne. (MGM, 1941)

Ann Carver's Profession. Gene Raymond broods over the fact that his wife (Fay Wray) is a successful lawyer, if an imperfect wife. (Columbia, 1933)

The Philadelphia Story. John Howard was about to marry Katherine Hepburn when ex-husband Cary Grant showed up, and the old spark was still alive. (MGM, 1940)

Flamingo Road. Zachary Scott lost his mustache in this Joan Crawford film, and later in it also lost his life. (Warner Brothers, 1949)

130

Born To Be Bad. The title referred to Joan Fontaine, Zachary Scott, and Joan Leslie. The role was not typical of Scott's style. (RKO, 1950)

Suddenly It's Spring. Fred MacMurray and Paulette Goddard were the stars, and Macdonald Carey (above) was the other man. (Paramount, 1947)

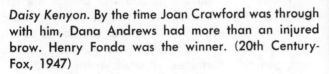

Daisy Kenyon. By the time Joan Crawford was through with him, Dana Andrews had more than an injured brow. Henry Fonda was the winner. (20th Century-Fox, 1947)

Sing, Baby Sing. Alice Faye was an aspiring actress and Adolphe Menjou an aging ham in this musical comedy. (20th Century-Fox, 1936)

played jazz trumpeters in pursuit of Paulette Goddard, and a wonderfully zany role in *Diary of a Chambermaid,* again with Miss Goddard.

But of all the charming, dashing actors to play Rival roles in light comedies or musicals, it would be difficult to find one more appealing—yet so clearly destined for Other Manhood—than Cesar Romero. His blinding smile, his sleek black hair (no less glamorous later when it turned silver), and his mildly dishonest manner all served him well in a seemingly endless succession of roles in which he sought to sway girls of irrefutable virtue, only to be foiled by Don Ameche, John Payne, Richard Greene, and other squeaky clean heroes.

A night club dancer in the 1920s, Romero didn't begin to click in Hollywood until the middle of the next decade. By the late 1930s, he was tremendously useful to 20th Century-Fox as the Other Man in a series of frothy musicals they were making then.

In 1938, it was *Happy Landing,* with Don Ameche happy that he landed Sonja Henie. The same year, Romero lost Henie again to Richard Greene in *My Lucky Star.* He was an equally unsuccessful suitor in three nonmusicals of that time: *Always Goodbye,* with Barbara Stanwyck and Herbert Marshall; *Wife, Husband, and*

Tierney. Price played a mad soap tycoon in *Champagne for Caesar,* which had Ronald Colman and Celeste Holm. And he was a convincing heavy in both *The Long Night,* with Henry Fonda and Barbara Bel Geddes, and *The Las Vegas Story,* with Jane Russell and Victor Mature.

A zanier Rival still was Burgess Meredith. A fine stage actor who made his Broadway mark in *Winterset,* he went to Hollywood to repeat that role for the screen. Soon after, he played a kind of one-man Greek chorus in *Idiot's Delight,* with Clark Gable and Norma Shearer. He was a whacky concert pianist who attracted Merle Oberon in the Lubitsch comedy *That Uncertain Feeling,* but she eventually decided in favor of Melvyn Douglas. In *Tom, Dick, and Harry,* he was one of three suitors after Ginger Rogers. The other two were George Murphy and Alan Marshall.

Meredith had a good funny Rival role in *Second Chorus,* in which he and Fred Astaire both

Turnabout. Two guys in a bed was one of the less startling innovations of this comedy. John Hubbard (William Gargan's bedmate, above) and Carole Landis switched psyches and clothes. And Adolphe Menjou was generally outraged. (United Artists, 1940)

One in a Million. Adolphe Menjou pleads with Sonja Henie, while Don Ameche and Jean Hersholt listen. Ameche won the One. (20th Century-Fox, 1936)

Friend, with Warner Baxter and Loretta Young; and *He Married His Wife*, with Joel McCrea and Nancy Kelly.

Then, back to musicals for a while: Romero wooed but didn't win Betty Grable in *Springtime in the Rockies*, with John Payne as the victor; he was the loser again and Payne the winner again in *Weekend In Havana*, with Alice Faye as the prize; and it was back to losing Sonja Henie (to Cornel Wilde) in *Wintertime*. The Faye-Payne-Romero triangle was repeated once more, in *The Great American Broadcast*, with the same results. By 1943, the leads had been switched to Betty Grable and George Montgomery, in *Coney Island*, but it was the same old Romero role.

After the war, it was more of the same. Dick Haymes won out over Romero in *Carnival in Costa Rica*, with Vera-Ellen as leading lady. In *That Lady in Ermine*, it was Ginger Rogers and Douglas Fairbanks, Jr., to the altar, and Romero left in the lurch. And in *Love That Brute*, Jean Peters preferred Paul Douglas to Romero.

By the late 1940s, Romero was parodying himself in successively ineffective films, turning evil swashbuckler in *Captain From Castile* (Tyrone Power and Jean Peters) and Brazilian bandito in

Leave Her to Heaven. Vincent Price (reading papers) first lost Gene Tierney to Cornel Wilde (taking oath) and then tried to convict him of killing her. (20th Century-Fox, 1945)

The Americano, with Glenn Ford. In the 1960s, Romero made several mock-villain appearances on the comic strip-type television series, "Batman."

The Rival category would hardly be complete without at least mention of some more actors:

Kent Taylor in *Ramona,* with Don Ameche and Loretta Young.

Jean-Pierre Aumont in *Lili,* with Leslie Caron and Mel Ferrer.

Broderick Crawford in *Born Yesterday,* with Judy Holliday and William Holden.

Francis Lederer in *A Woman of Distinction,* with Rosalind Russell and Ray Milland.

Aldo Ray in *Miss Sadie Thompson,* with Rita Hayworth and Jose Ferrer.

Plus Claude Rains, Barry Sullivan, Wendell Corey, John Howard, Brian Donlevy, Barry Sullivan, Donald Woods, Jeff Chandler, Robert Ryan, Richard Carlson, Richard Greene, Arthur Kennedy, and, of course, Sonny Tufts.

From David Niven to Cesar Romero, from Robert Young to Robert Cummings, a succession of actors has breathed life into the role of Rival.

The Comedy of Terrors. Turning to mock horror, a couple of old pros extended their careers. Vincent Price and Basil Rathbone, two veteran villains, were joined by Peter Lorre and Boris Karloff in this exercise. (American-International, 1963)

Without them no triangle could have been complete.

Besides making a nice living and sometimes using this experience as a base for more rewarding film careers, they helped to shape the style and scope of four decades of American movies—not to mention moulding the tastes and preferences of audiences.

With certain exceptions (which will be examined next) the ground rules of these Hollywood movies were pretty rigid and confining. One of the basic rules was that no matter how attractive the Rival might be, the leading lady always decided in favor of the male star.

This was even so in the numerous films that involved the sudden reappearance—after being presumed dead—of a spouse (*Suzy, The Dark Angel, Today We Live, My Favorite Wife, Too Many Husbands, Tomorrow Is Forever, Move Over Darling*). The moment the spouse turned up, you knew the Rival's scenes were limited.

Incidentally, if any lingering doubts should remain as to the power of the motion picture medium's influence over human emotions, consider the pathetic spectacle of all those wives, mothers, and sweethearts of men listed as Missing in Action in Indochina. Against all advice (even from the Pentagon) they persist in clinging to the hope that somehow, somewhere, their men are alive and will turn up, if only those nasty Communists will cooperate. And why shouldn't they? After all, forty years of movies have helped to perpetuate the magical myth of spouses given up for dead who miraculously reappear. Dozens of movies, good, bad, and indifferent, have used this particular fairy tale as the basis of their plots. And dozens of otherwise eligible Rivals have thus been eliminated.

Tom, Dick, and Harry. Ginger Rogers toyed with the affections of three swains in this comedy: George Murphy, Burgess Meredith, and Alan Marshall, all experienced losers. (RKO, 1941)

Idiot's Delight. Burgess Meredith played a despairing pacifist in this one. With him above are Pat Paterson, Peter Wiles, Skeets Gallagher, Charles Coburn, and Clark Gable. (Missing is Gable's co-star, Norma Shearer.) (MGM, 1939)

Coney Island. George Montgomery and Betty Grable were the love birds this time, and Cesar Romero was left in the sand. (20th Century-Fox, 1943)

Second Chorus. Burgess Meredith and Fred Astaire were dance band musicians battling over Paulette Goddard. Meredith was second trumpet. (Paramount, 1940)

The Leather Saint. Paul Douglas and Jody Lawrence flank a silvery-maned Cesar Romero, who was still playing The Rival. (Paramount, 1956)

Winter Time. Sonja Henie danced with Cesar Romero, a hardened rival by this time in his career. (20th Century-Fox, 1943)

Julia Misbehaves. Cesar Romero and Greer Garson cuddle while Walter Pidgeon stews. But everything turned out fine for Garson-Pidgeon fans. (MGM, 1948)

Ramona. Kent Taylor, a standard Rival, loved Loretta Young, but she preferred Don Ameche in this romance. (20th Century-Fox, 1936)

Born Yesterday. Judy Holliday switched from Broderick Crawford to William Holden in this classic Garson Kanin comedy. (Columbia, 1950)

140

Lili. Leslie Caron was awed by Jean-Pierre Aumont, but Mel Ferrer (left) came from behind to win the girl. The friend is Kurt Kasznar. (MGM, 1953)

A Woman of Distinction. That's Francis Lederer with Rosalind Russell above, but she dumped him in favor of Ray Milland. (Columbia, 1950)

Miss Sadie Thompson. This version of the Somerset Maugham story had Rita Hayworth in the title role, Aldo Ray as a marine, and Jose Ferrer as the Rev. Mr. Davidson. (Columbia, 1954)

Crime without Passion. Claude Rains, a master rival, with Margo, in an early Rains success. (Paramount, 1934)

Now, Voyager. Claude Rains played a sympathetic psychiatrist in this Bette Davis drama. Paul Henreid was the man she loved in vain. (Warner Brothers, 1942)

Let's Do It Again. This rehash of *The Awful Truth* didn't even come close to the original. Jane Wyman and Ray Milland were the divorcing couple, Aldo Ray the square rival. (Columbia, 1953)

And Now Tomorrow. Alan Ladd and Loretta Young were the stars, Barry Sullivan the extra man. Also above is Cecil Kellaway. (Paramount, 1944)

The Wild North. Wendell Corey's life was saved by Stewart Granger in this snowbound adventure. Cyd Charisse was the girl. (MGM, 1952)

Destry Rides Again. Marlene Dietrich shies away from Brian Donlevy. Destry (the winner) was played by James Stewart. (Universal, 1939)

Wonder Man. Donald Woods was Danny Kaye's luckless rival in this musical comedy. The girl was Virginia Mayo, not shown above. (RKO, 1945)

Ice Palace. Robert Ryan, a veteran rival, with Carolyn Jones. The leading man of this drama was Richard Burton. (Warner Brothers, 1960)

Sword in the Desert. Marta Toren (above) and Dana Andrews were the stars of Jeff Chandler's first picture, a drama about helping refugees out of Europe. (Universal, 1949)

The Blue Veil. Richard Carlson won some, lost some in his film career. With him above is Jane Wyman, who lost at love and turned to nursing. (Columbia, 1947)

Little Old New York. Fred MacMurray, Alice Faye, and Richard Greene in another of those pseudo-historical dramas. (20th Century-Fox, 1940)

Nevada Smith. Arthur Kennedy played friends, rivals, and some leads. In this one, he was Steve McQueen's chaingang friend. (Paramount, 1966)

Miss Susie Slagle's. Sonny Tufts and Joan Caulfield starred in this one, a rare role for Tufts: he was the leading man. (Paramount, 1945)

5
The Lucky Friend

During his years as a producer at Metro-Gold-wyn-Mayer, the biggest of the big studios, the late David O. Selznick had been responsible for many of that company's top productions, including *Dinner at Eight, Dancing Lady, David Copperfield, Anna Karenina,* and *A Tale of Two Cities.*

He left MGM in 1936 to form his own company, Selznick International, and spent the next two decades as his own boss. The list of his pictures is lengthy, but its quality can best be indicated by mentioning that it included such outstanding films as *A Star Is Born, Nothing Sacred, Intermezzo, Rebecca,* and the formidable *Gone with the Wind.*

His relations with MGM after his departure from that studio remained cordial. He had married Irene Mayer, daughter of the MGM boss, Louis B. Mayer. In 1944, MGM was making *Gaslight,* based on a hit stage play that had already been filmed in England. (The English film was later released here as *Angel Street.*)

Selznick had no part in this film, but had a great interest in it. Two of his contract stars, Ingrid Bergman and Joseph Cotten, were on loan to MGM to star in the picture, along with Charles Boyer. In those days, producers who had stars under contract made handsome profits by loaning out their stars to other studios for particular

films, the compensation for these loan-outs going to the contract holder rather than the player, who of course continued to get his regular salary during the loan-out period.

So it was that when *Gaslight,* produced by Arthur Hornblow, Jr., and directed by George Cukor, was finished shooting, Louis B. Mayer invited his son-in-law to view the film and offer his comments on it.

Selznick accepted the invitation—both to look at the movie and to offer his criticisms. Being a prolific memo writer, he ventured a number of opinions and suggestions that he felt would strengthen an already good film. Some of these had to do with clarification of story, others urged retakes of certain scenes for possible better results.

On one particular point, he felt very strongly: Selznick believed that even the merest suggestion of a romantic link between Ingrid Bergman and Joseph Cotten was a grave error in judgment. Cotten played a Scotland Yard detective whose curiosity finally entrapped Boyer and rescued Miss Bergman. The hint that, after this, Cotten and Ingrid should begin any sort of personal relationship struck Selznick as all wrong. He felt that the characters barely knew each other, would hardly have had a chance to become interested in each other, and furthermore that the character played by Miss Bergman wouldn't be inclined to suddenly fall in love with the character played by Cotten.

Had Selznick made the film, he no doubt would have followed his own instincts on such matters. But MGM had its own ideas and men like Cukor and Hornblow, Jr., obviously had their own dramatic and commercial sets of values.

In any case, although MGM took up some of Selznick's suggestions, on this one the studio chose to ignore his advice and the film, as released, still contained a hint of possible future romance between the two characters in question.

The fact is Selznick was spitting against the wind and his attempt to buck an old and hallowed Hollywood tradition was doomed. That

Gaslight. Ingrid Bergman, threatened by Charles Boyer, attracted the sympathy of detective Joseph Cotten, who hung around and won. (MGM, 1941)

tradition is the basis for the next category of Hollywood's Other Men—the Lucky Friend.

Just as it was and is necessary to have a Rival (or at least a Friend) to complete the triangle that is the basis of Hollywood romance, so in certain circumstances was it necessary to have a Lucky Friend.

The circumstances are simple enough. Rule One is the "satisfying ending," which almost always means a happy ending. But on those rare occasions when an unhappy ending was really essential to the story, a ray of hope must still be indicated—simply to avoid leaving the audience disappointed. ("Word of mouth" being regarded as a valuable form of advertising, a disappointed moviegoer could not be depended upon to recommend the film to a friend.) If the leading man turned out to be a cad, theif, killer, or coward, or even if, while remaining admirable, it became necessary in the story for him to die—usually by performing some selfless act to save the lives of others—it was still considered "unsatisfying" for the heroine to be left manless.

Usually, the simplest way around this was to have a second man—the Other Man, in a sense—hanging about the periphery of the story, with very little to do, until the hero was carted away, dead or alive. Then the heroine, in her grief and loneliness, would turn to the broad male shoulder nearest her, upon which to vent her bitter tears. The mere presence of such a shoulder hinted that soon—maybe not tomorrow, but soon—she would find solace in this strong, hitherto forgettable male whose presence in the film until now was more or less pointless.

Gaslight was a good example, though by no means either the first or the last. Charles Boyer played a suave, superficially charming menace. Married to the beauteous Ingrid, his plot was to drive her mad so he could get his hands on her jewels. The film's suspense built up as the audience began to realize that Miss Bergman's sanity and life were being jeopardized by her supposedly loving husband. She was saved, ultimately, by the curiosity of detective Cotten, and the evil husband's plot was foiled.

But MGM insisted in leaving in that bit of a suggestion that Ingrid, so recently relieved of the terror of a husband she clearly didn't know very well, is about to leap into a relationship with an-

Sleep, My Love. Robert Cummings was suspicious of Don Ameche's treatment of Claudette Colbert. Naturally, his hunch paid off. (United Artists, 1947)

other comparative stranger. However illogical that may seem (to us as it did to Selznick) it was apparently preferable to the grim prospect of having Ingrid go out into the world unescorted.

The Lucky Friend, therefore, can be defined as a man whose involvement in the story may be (indeed, often is) minimal, but whose presence at the denouement is vital. He is usually not the dashing young man who brought our heroine to the ball, but rather the stolid, reliable fellow who

Dial M for Murder. This famous Hitchcock thriller had Ray Milland trying to kill his wife, Grace Kelly. But Robert Cummings eventually saw through the whole thing. (Warner Brothers, 1954)

silently takes her home after everything goes wrong, and then, implicitly, presses his new advantage.

Unlike the Rival, he must not appear to be competing for our heroine's hand. Or, if he does, most of the clues along the way should indicate that he doesn't stand a chance of winning her—until after the more appealing hero gets killed, is revealed to be a bounder, or in some other way comes a cropper.

One other point about the Lucky Friend should be noted. Unlike the average Funny Friend or Nice Friend, the Lucky Friend need not be a buddy of the hero's. Often, his function is more easily carried out if he is a friend (or, at least, a casual acquaintance) of the heroine's.

Most of the Hollywood actors who have played Lucky Friends have already been referred to in this book—as Rivals, Nice Friends, or leading men. A few remained relatively unknown, but for their one or two chances to play Lucky Friend.

Robert Cummings, a consummate Rival and perennial star, played Lucky Friend in two films,

Night Must Fall. Robert Montgomery was the psychopathic killer, Rosalind Russell was attracted to him. But Lucky Friend Alan Marshall was still around when they carted Montgomery off to jail. (MGM, 1937)

one of them quite similar to *Gaslight*. This was in 1947, in a picture called *Sleep My Love*, with Claudette Colbert and Don Ameche.

This time, Ameche was married to Claudette and trying to drive her mad. Poor Claudette, according to Ameche's sinister scheme, was supposed to become so unhinged that she'd take her own life, leaving Ameche free to link up with the comely Hazel Brooks. But the plot misfired, of course, and not only did Ameche get his comeuppance, but Claudette had Robert Cummings, her Lucky Friend, to turn to in the final scene.

Cummings's other Lucky Friend role was in a more famous film, *Dial M for Murder*, directed by Alfred Hitchcock and starring Ray Milland and Grace Kelly. In this story, Milland, a bounder in financial straits, hires a killer to do away with his wife (Grace) so he can inherit her money. But instead, she kills the killer in self-defense and then detective John Williams sets about the task of unraveling the mystery. Cummings is around as a visiting ex-boy friend of Grace's and, unlike other Lucky Friends, he is actually instrumental in solving the crime and getting Milland locked up. In fairness, he deserved to win Grace.

Psychopath roles have often been attractive for

A Rage in Heaven. Robert Montgomery was bananas again, convinced his wife, Ingrid Bergman, loved George Sanders. When he finally did himself in, Sanders was around to console Ingrid. (MGM, 1941)

Laura. Clifton Webb and Gene Tierney watch Dana Andrews punch Vincent Price. Detective Andrews solved the crime and won the girl. (20th Century-Fox, 1944)

actors, particularly actors determined to prove they can break away from silly playboy parts and do something more "serious."

Thus, in 1937, Robert Montgomery persuaded MGM to let him play Danny, the twisted murderer of the Emlyn Williams play, *Night Must Fall.* The glib, charming Danny moves into the home of tyrannical Dame May Whitty and flatters her into making him her pet. The old woman's niece, Rosalind Russell, is at once frightened and infatuated by him. Meanwhile, her bland, emotionless suitor, Alan Marshall, fades into the background. Eventually, Danny is revealed to be

a mad killer (the head of an earlier victim is kept in a hat box under his bed) and Lucky Friend Marshall materializes in time to take Roz away from all this.

Montgomery tried to do it all again, a few years later, in a far less successful movie called *A Rage in Heaven.* This time he was married to Ingrid Bergman but wrongly suspected Ingrid and his friend, George Sanders, of being in love. His twisted mind led him to another course: he killed himself but left phoney evidence to indicate that Sanders had done him in. In time, the true facts were brought to light and Lucky Friend

153

Shadow of a Doubt. Joseph Cotten joined the would-be killers in this Hitchcock film, and friendly detective Macdonald Carey was on hand to console Teresa Wright. Universal, 1943)

Sanders won his freedom—and Ingrid.

Police officers and doctors tend to make good Lucky Friends. Besides Joseph Cotten in *Gaslight*, there was Dana Andrews in *Laura*. This clever Otto Preminger film had Gene Tierney in the title role, plus a fine cast that included Clifton Webb, Vincent Price, and Judith Anderson.

Andrews was the detective assigned to solve the "murder" of beautiful Miss Tierney, whom he'd never met. By the end of the movie, he (1) finds that Laura—or Gene—is still alive, (2) traps Clifton Webb as the killer (of another girl), and (3) falls in love with Laura and she with him. That's pretty nice work for a Lucky Friend.

In *Shadow of a Doubt,* an Alfred Hitchcock film of 1943, we see growing evidence that Joseph Cotten, the unbalanced uncle this time around, is planning to kill his niece, Teresa Wright. Lucky policeman Macdonald Carey has little to do, but he wins the girl.

Then there was Glenn Langan, an actor whose fame was somewhat limited, despite his appearances in such movies as *Forever Amber, Margie,*

Four Jills in a Jeep, and *The Snake Pit.* It was in *Dragonwyck,* a Gothic-type suspense drama with Gene Tierney and Vincent Price, that Langan played a doctor who turned out to be a Lucky Friend. For reasons too silly to go into, Gene defies her strict parents and allows herself to be swept off her feet by wealthy Vincent. Ensconced in his spooky Hudson River mansion, she begins to go bananas under the evil influence of her sneering husband. But the good doctor (Langan) turns up in the nick of time to check her pulse and win her heart.

Another surprise winner—or Lucky Friend— was Dick Foran, in *Rangers of Fortune.* This 1940 Western was rather conventional except in one sense: the star (Fred MacMurray) didn't get the girl. He was engaged to Patricia Morrison, but he got all involved in Texas and by the time he got home the lady had decided to marry Friend Foran.

Franchot Tone, that evergreen playboy, drew the Lucky Friend role in a couple of early films. One of these was *Suzy,* which starred Cary Grant and Jean Harlow. Tone is Harlow's first husband, reported killed in the war. She then marries Grant a philandering flyer who gets involved with a German spy (Benita Hume) and dies in disgrace. Then Tone returns from the dead (Lucky, eh?), reclaims Harlow, and juggles the

Dragonwyck. Vincent Price made life hell for Gene Tierney, but friendly doctor Glenn Langan (above) nursed her back to health and outlasted Price. (20th Century-Fox, 1946)

Wings of the Navy. George Brent was the star, but he yielded Olivia de Havilland to his younger brother, played by John Payne. (Warner Brothers, 1939)

Rangers of Fortune. Fred MacMurray got so involved with the Texas Rangers that he missed his scheduled wedding to Patricia Morrison, who simply switched to Dick Foran. (Paramount, 1940)

Suzy. Franchot Tone was lucky to be in a film in which Cary Grant got killed. Result: Tone ended up with Jean Harlow. (MGM, 1936)

The Bride Wore Red. Joan Crawford set her cap for snobbish Robert Young, who spurned her. She settled for the folksy postman, Franchot Tone. (MGM, 1937)

evidence to make it look as if Grant had died heroically.

Tone got lucky again in *The Bride Wore Red*, a 1937 pastiche with Joan Crawford and Robert Young. In this Ruritanian romance, little Joan has a rich (and manifestly eccentric) admirer who finances a vacation for her at a ritzy Tyrolean resort. Putting on phoney airs, she attracts socialite Robert Young and befriends the village postman—Franchot Tone, of all people. In the end, Young realizes she isn't of his aristocratic world and rejects her, whereupon Joan settles for Lucky Friend Tone, content to live an honest life of simplicity and rural free delivery.

Jeffey Lynn lived a charmed life as Lucky Friend in several pictures (although he was singularly unlucky as poet Joyce Kilmer in *The Fighting 69th*). In *All This and Heaven Too*, a popular 1940 drama, Jeffrey played a young min-

ister who first meets Bette Davis aboard a Channel boat bound for France. Bette tells him she is going to be governess to the children of a wealthy Duc (Charles Boyer) and Duchess (Barbara O'Neil). The story leaves Lynn and follows Bette through some soapy adventures—the jealousy of the demented Duchess, an incipient romance with Boyer, the mysterious murder of the Duchess, a public scandal (after which Bette is absolved), and the suicide of the Duc. Wiser but not notably older, Bette finally returns to America to take a position and then learns that the minister from the first reel (Jeffrey Lynn) got her the needed job. When he comes to visit her, you know she has new hope and he's become a Lucky Friend.

The Roaring Twenties was an effective gangster film starring James Cagney, Priscilla Lane, and Humphrey Bogart. Jeffrey Lynn, Cagney and Bogart are World War One buddies, then go

156

their separate ways: Bogart into crime, Cagney not far behind, and Lynn into law. Cagney falls for Priscilla, helps launch her singing career. She meets Lynn, who is now Cagney's lawyer. Cagney steps aside so Priscilla and Jeffrey can marry. Repeal of prohibition puts Cagney on the skids, but, unaccountably, not Bogart. When Lynn becomes an assistant district attorney he goes after Bogart, who wants to kill him. But Cagney, a bum but a noble one, eliminates both Bogart and himself, thus leaving New York a cleaner place in which Priscilla and Lucky Friend Lynn can live.

Lynn's other Lucky Friend experience was a kind of Daily Double, in that it involved two films (the second a "sequel") and yielded two Lucky Friends. The films were *Four Daughters* and *Four Wives*.

Now, if you can keep the players straight, here goes: Priscilla Lane loves Jeffrey Lynn, but so does her sister, Gale Page, who is quietly loved by Dick Foran. Enter John Garfield as the sardonic defeatist who falls in love with Priscilla. When Gale is quietly heartbroken over losing Lynn to Priscilla, Dick Foran lends a muscular shoulder for her to cry on. Consolation blooms

The Roaring Twenties. Tough guy James Cagney eliminated bad guy Bogart, who had been threatening Jeffrey Lynn. He also eliminated himself, leaving Priscilla Lane to Lynn. (Warner Brothers, 1939)

Four Wives. Gale Page and Lane Sisters Rosemary, Lola, and Priscilla matched up with Dick Foran, Frank McHugh, Eddie Albert, and Jeffrey Lynn. This tidy, happy ending was set up by the drama in the film's predecessor, *Four Daughters.* (Warner Brothers, 1939)

The Charge of the Light Brigade. Brothers Patric Knowles and Errol Flynn both loved Olivia de Havilland. Flynn charged away to history, leaving Patric to Olivia. (Warner Brothers, 1936)

into love and Lucky Friend Foran wins Gale.

Meanwhile, back at the main plot, Priscilla, out of sympathy for her sister, jilts Lynn and runs off with the gloomy Garfield. But gloom is a way of life for Garfield, and he soon realizes he is doomed to failure—except in one thing: he succeeds at suicide. After that, Jeffrey Lynn turns up again, but the story sort of hangs there.

In the sequel, *Four Wives*, Gale Page is married to Dick Foran, Lola Lane to Frank Mc-Hugh, and Rosemary Lane marries Eddie Albert. That leaves Priscilla, who discovers she is carrying the dead Garfield's baby. But Jeffrey Lynn is not about to lose out again. He finally becomes Lucky Friend Number Two and marries Priscilla.

Patric Knowles, often a Bellamy-type Rival and occasionally a leading man, turned Lucky Friend in *The Charge of the Light Brigade*, an early Errol Flynn swashbuckler. In this one, Major Flynn is engaged to Olivia de Havilland, who has secretly fallen in love with Flynn's younger brother, Patric Knowles. (Miss de Havilland seems to have been in a rut. She switches brothers, you may remember, in *Wings of the Navy*, going from O'Brien to Payne.) Despite her heart's desire, the fair Olivia is duty bound to marry Flynn. The rest of the story bore so little resemblance to the truth as to be ludicrous (a far less romanticized version of *The Charge of the Light Brigade* was

Midnight Lace. Husband Rex Harrison was trying to kill wife Doris Day, but kindly neighbor John Gavin (above) rescued her. (Universal, 1960)

made by England's Tony Richardson some thirty-two years later), but the point here is that Flynn got himself killed in the Charge, leaving Olivia to Lucky Friend/Brother Knowles.

Midnight Lace, a 1960 Doris Day opus, offered a handy Lucky Friend role to John Gavin. In this London-based thriller, Miss Day gave us a symphony of screaming as suspects kept being tossed in like so many red herrings. The man trying to murder her turned out to be her husband (Rex Harrison) and the fellow who rescued her was that inoffensive neighbor, played by Mr. Gavin. In true Lucky Friend fashion, he not only quieted Miss Day's hysterical tears, but left one and all with the distinct impression that Doris would be well protected from there on in.

Humphrey Bogart was responsible for setting up a Lucky Friend in one of his most famous films, *Casablanca*. This wartime drama had Bogart and Ingrid Bergman as former lovers who meet again in Casablanca in the dark days when it still looked as if Hitler might win the war. By now, of course, Ingrid is reunited with husband Paul Henreid (who was believed dead but—surprise!—turned up alive after Bogart deserted Ingrid in Paris). Henreid is now a leader of the underground resistance. But when Ingrid and Bogart see each other, it's plain the old romance is not dead. There's a great deal of intrigue and double-dealing before the ending, in which Bogart provides the papers that will allow Henreid and Miss Bergman to escape the Nazis and get to Lisbon, where Henreid can continue his resistance work. Although it's true that Henreid was married to Bergman in this film and Bogart was the other man, the stars of the film were Bogart and Bergman, so for Henreid to win the girl—and over Bogart, at that—certainly qualifies him as a Lucky Friend.

Eight years later, Bogart did it again. This time the film was titled *Sirocco* and it had to do with Middle Eastern intrigue in 1925. Bogart is selling guns to the Arabs in French-occupied Damascus. His business is stymied by a colonel of French Intelligence (Lee J. Cobb) but Bogart gets even by luring Cobb's mistress (Marta Toren) away from him. Later, Bogart is persuaded to try to rescue Cobb, who has been captured by the Arabs. Bogart succeeds in springing Cobb, but pays with his own life, leaving Lucky Friend

Casablanca. Humphrey Bogart still carried a torch for Ingrid Bergman, but realized he had to help her husband, Paul Henreid, to continue his underground work against the Nazis. The man in uniform above is Claude Rains. (Warner Brothers, 1942)

Sirocco. Humphrey Bogart and Lee J. Cobb were both in love with Marta Toren, but in the end only Cobb was left alive to console her. (Columbia, 1951)

Sabrina. In this comedy, Audrey Hepburn was all set to marry millionaire William Holden, but eventually switched to his lucky brother, Humphrey Bogart. (Paramount, 1954)

Torch Song. Michael Wilding was Joan Crawford's blind accompanist, but she finally chose him over Gig Young. (MGM, 1953)

Cobb to return to the arms of Miss Toren.

One more Bogart movie bears mentioning, because this time Bogart turned out to be the Lucky Friend. This was *Sabrina,* a Billy Wilder comedy based on a successful Broadway play. (The play was called *Sabrina Fair,* which was a girl's name, but the movie types dropped the second word because they feared moviegoers might expect a movie about a carnival.) Audrey Hepburn played Sabrina, the daughter of a chauffeur to a wealthy family. Audrey falls for William Holden, the likable younger son of the wealthy family, and sets out to win him. But the family disapproves and assigns Bogart, the stuffy older brother, to distract Audrey. He does such a good job of it that they end up marrying. Since the three stars—Bogart, Hepburn, and Holden—were on equal footing, it might not seem illogical that Bogart should win, except that Bogart was by now past his peak as a romantic star, whereas Holden was still twenty years younger and seemed the more likely winner.

Michael Wilding, that habitual loser, got lucky in *Torch Song,* a 1953 Joan Crawford movie in which he was pitted against Gig Young and had the additional handicap of being blind.

Miss Crawford plays a tough Broadway singer and Wilding is her blind accompanist. Wilding,

whose hearing is perfectly okay, keeps criticizing Joan's singing, and she keeps arguing with him. Hungry for true love, Joan is romanced by dashing Gig Young, but in time she realizes he's not for her. Not until another woman (Dorothy Patrick) shows some interest in Wilding does Joan wake up to the fact that she really loves her sightless accompanist. Anybody who can win Joan Crawford away from Gig Young, despite being blind, must be regarded as a Lucky Friend.

The same Miss Crawford (who, incidentally, appears to have made more movies than anybody) was involved in yet another triangle in *Goodbye My Fancy,* in which Robert Young was the leading man and Frank Lovejoy the Lucky Friend. Joan is a congresswoman this time, returning to the college from which she'd once been expelled (for holding radical views) to receive an honorary degree. For her the visit also means a reunion with her former love (Young), now president of

Goodbye, My Fancy. Joan Crawford eventually realized that Robert Young was not the man she remembered, so Frank Lovejoy moved into the vacuum. (Warner Brothers, 1951)

the college. During the visit to her alma mater, Joan becomes aware that Young has changed. Instead of the fearless idealist of her romantic memory, he has become a stodgy, submissive pawn of the conservative school trustees. Fortunately for Joan, Frank Lovejoy, as a photographer with a yen for her, has been lurking about snapping pictures and periodically declaring his love for her. In the end, Joan dumps the stuffy college president and turns to the Lucky Leica addict.

Mildred Pierce. Indulgent mother Joan Crawford's marriage to Bruce Bennett broke up. But when all the shooting was over (Ann Blyth killed Zachary Scott) there was a hint that Joan and Bruce might try again. (Warner Brothers, 1945)

Herman Brix may not seem like an especially euphonius name for a Hollywood film actor, but it served the man who owned it for a time. Blessed with the required physique, he made two Tarzan features in the 1930s (somewhere between Johnny Weissmuller and Buster Crabbe) but eventually realized that if he was to make it in films he'd have to do two things: put on some clothes and change his name. His new name was Bruce Bennett, but neither it nor his new wardrobe helped him in his quest for stardom.

As Bennett, he played supporting roles in A Stolen Life, with Bette Davis and Glenn Ford; Nora Prentiss, with Ann Sheridan and Robert Alda; Dream Wife, with Cary Grant and Deborah Kerr; and Sudden Fear, with Joan Crawford and Jack Palance. In none of these was he memorable.

But he made another movie with Joan Crawford, which turned out to be her biggest hit and won her an Academy Award. This was Mildred Pierce, in 1945, and even though Bennett's role was the least impressive of the three leading male parts, he finally fell into the Lucky Friend category.

Mildred Pierce (Miss Crawford) is an ambitious lady who neglects her husband (Bennett) and spoils her daughter (Ann Blyth). The marriage goes on the rocks and Bennett goes off into the wings. Mildred meets nice guy Jack Carson, who helps her open a small restaurant. He also introduces her to Zachary Scott, a snobbish cad, who begins playing around with daughter Ann, even though he knows Mildred is falling for him. Mama Mildred fails to see any fault in her selfish daughter until it's too late. The daughter murders Scott, and Mildred (Joan) tries to protect her offspring by confessing to the murder herself. However, justice triumphs: Ann Blyth goes to prison for murder and Mildred Pierce starts thinking about going back to her husband, who's hardly been seen since the first reel—Lucky Bruce Bennett.

David Niven was a kind of Lucky Friend in The Dawn Patrol, a 1938 melodrama about World War One flyers and the movie, if memory serves, that spawned that deathless line: "You can't send that boy up in a crate like this."

The Dawn Patrol (first made in 1930) had to do with the heroic exploits of the British Royal Flying Corps. Basil Rathbone is the squadron

The Dawn Patrol. Errol Flynn decided to take a suicide mission originally scheduled for David Niven, thus leaving Niven as the highest ranking survivor. (Warner Brothers, 1938)

The Bishop's Wife. However charming Cary Grant may be, the fact that he was really a ghost gave David Niven a fighting chance (or a lucky break) in keeping Loretta Young. (RKO, 1947)

commander, the "butcher" responsible for sending up boys like this in crates like that. When he is promoted and transferred, the command is turned over to Errol Flynn. It is Flynn's unfortunate duty to send David Niven's younger brother to his death on a mission, thereby putting a considerable strain on the friendship between Flynn and Niven. To prove his bravery (or salve his conscience) Flynn takes on a dangerous mission originally scheduled for Niven. Flynn gets himself killed and the film ends with Niven taking over the squadron. The movie had no love interest, but since Niven was the only one of the leads still alive and kicking at the conclusion, he must be awarded the Lucky Friend ribbon.

Niven was lucky in another sense in a 1948 comedy called *The Bishop's Wife*. Niven was the bishop of the title and Loretta Young was his wife. In the role of an angel who drops by (or down) to help Niven through various difficulties was Cary Grant. Angel or no angel, Grant is still Grant, and the bishop's wife can be forgiven for being attracted to him. Niven can be considered lucky in that Grant was required to go back upstairs and play his harp rather than stay down at the bishop's house for who knows what sort of extra-spiritual hanky-panky.

Van Johnson got lucky in *A Guy Names Joe*, which had Irene Dunne and Spencer Tracy as stars. This time, Tracy was a flyer who had gone up to that wild blue yonder up yonder, but came back to help make Van a better flyer. If Niven was lucky to be in a Cary Grant picture in which Grant was a ghost, the same applies to Van Johnson with respect to Spencer Tracy.

But first place among Lucky Friends in movie history must go to Donald Woods, and on the basis of only one particular film.

Woods, a capable second-lead and B-picture leading man for many years, was best known in the 1930s and 1940s. He was a rival of sorts to Danny Kaye in *Wonder Man*. He had a pleasant if innocuous role in *Watch on the Rhine*, with Bette Davis and Paul Lukas. He was a prop in *Night and Day*, which had Cary Grant masquerading as Cole Porter. He was an aide to Paul Muni in *The Story of Louis Pasteur*, and he supported Fredric March in *Anthony Adverse*.

But his sole claim to Lucky Friend fame came in 1935 in the MGM movie version of the Dickens classic, *A Tale of Two Cities*, in which he played Charles Darnay to Ronald Colman's Sydney Carton.

Darnay, for the benefit of those who were absent from English Lit. class that day, is a French aristocrat (but one of the nice ones) doomed to execution by the nasty revolutionaries who have overrun France in the days of Robespierre. Darnay is betrothed to Lucie Manette (Elizabeth Allan), who is also loved by the poetic but boozy Sydney Carton.

In one of the most noble sacrifices in all of literature, Carton arranges Darnay's escape from prison, then, posing as Darnay, he goes to the guillotine, intoning those heart-breaking lines: "It is a far, far better thing I do than I have ever done; it is a far, far better rest that I go to than I have ever known."

Zonk goes the guillotine, and into the waiting arms of Elizabeth Allan goes Donald Woods. That's what you call a Lucky Friend.

A Tale of Two Cities. Ronald Colman as Sydney Carton made the supreme sacrifice in the Dickens classic, going to the guillotine in place of Charles Darnay (Donald Woods, center) so the latter could marry Elizabeth Allan. The aide above is Walter Catlett. (MGM, 1935)

A Guy Named Joe. Spencer Tracy was a ghost returned to coach young pilots like Van Johnson, Barry Nelson, and Don DeFore. It was Van who won Irene Dunne. (MGM, 1943)

6

Bing's Friends, Foes and Foils

In the past ten years, he has made only two movies, the last one in 1966. But he still stars in his own annual television show at Christmas and occasionally turns up on his friends' "specials."

He is a tycoon (frozen foods, sports, movie and television productions, etc.) and a quiet supporter of conservative causes. He lends his support and his talents to various charitable organizations.

He is a private person. Long before it was fashionable to do so, he moved away from the Hollywood area—and not to "chic" Palm Springs but to the San Francisco area.

As he approaches seventy, he can look back on one of the most remarkable careers in entertainment any man ever lived through. With the possible exception of Chaplin, he was for many years the best-known entertainer in the world. He sold hundreds of millions of records. His recording of "White Christmas" alone has sold more than thirty million copies—a figure still unmatched by any other recording ever made.

He appeared in some sixty films. Ten of those (made between 1944 and 1963) have returned to their distributors a total of some sixty-five million dollars from theater rentals in North America. The actual box-office dollars paid out would likely more than double that figure. And that would still not include money these movies earned in Europe and elsewhere in the world—or from television exposure.

He won an Academy Award as the best film actor of the year in 1944, and twice was chosen best actor by the New York Film Critics.

But Bing Crosby would be the last person in the world to describe himself as a serious actor. Not that he indulges in false modesty. But he has a realistic way of appraising himself and his abilities. He has been described (by himself and others) as a "light comedian," and most critics have commented on his flair for making everything he does seem so easy and natural.

Perhaps more so than most other stars, Crosby has almost always played himself—an easy-going, relaxed, likable man with a flair for literate turns of phrase and a veneer of coolness that effectively disguises the degree of skill and professionalism that go into his work.

From the start, people liked him, reacted favorably to him because he seemed so ordinary, so like them. He was not extraordinarily handsome or graceful, his singing seemed so effortless that anyone could delude himself into thinking he could do as well. And yet this resulted in affection rather than resentment.

With few exceptions—and those mostly in the later years of his career as film star—the stories of his movies were inconsequential, flimsy, inoffensive. For the most part they were vehicles for him. His main business was to sing four or five songs, have a little fun and win the girl over lud-

Bing Crosby. This portrait is just forty years old, taken when Bing had completed the 1934 film, *She Loves Me Not*.

icrously inadequate opposition.

The roles he played reflected the essential Crosby personality: down-at-the-heels song writers, racetrack dreamers, ne'er do well drifters, disinherited playboys, out of work song and dance men, itinerant musicians, or genial roustabouts. Nothing ever seemed urgent to the characters Crosby played, and somehow that, too, was appealing.

For the record, in the sixty-odd pictures he made during the almost four decades when he was a superstar, he was never a Funny Friend, a Nice Friend, Lucky Friend, or a Rival. He was a leading man. Period.

In some of his biggest films, he appeared with such nonname leading ladies as Mary Carlisle, Nancy Olsen, and Colleen Gray. But he also worked opposite such distinguished stars as Ingrid Bergman, Jane Wyman, Carole Lombard, Joan Fontaine, Mary Martin, and Grace Kelly.

(It may also be worth noting that a number of Bing's films—whether he had a say in the matter or not—evolved from the works of such reputable authors as James Barrie, Mark Twain,

Too Much Harmony. Jack Oakie was Bing's friendly rival for Judith Allen in this early Crosby film. (Paramount, 1933)

Mississippi. Gambler Paul Hurst isn't too sure about the way W. C. Fields is dealing—and he's right. (Paramount, 1935)

Booth Tarkington, O. Henry, and Clifford Odets.)

Among the veteran directors who made three or more films each with Crosby were Frank Tuttle, Norman Taurog, Elliott Nugent, Edward Sutherland, and Victor Schertzinger. He also worked with such top-name directors as Frank Capra, Leo McCarey, Billy Wilder, Lewis Milestone, and Raoul Walsh.

Frank Capra, who directed Crosby twice (in *Riding High* and *Here Comes the Groom*) apparently approached the first encounter with some trepidation—based largely on second-hand reports he'd heard about Crosby's lackadaisical attitude toward work. But he later paid lavish tribute to Bing's cooperative spirit, his versatility,

and his ability to improve on written dialogue, terming Crosby a masterful ad libber.*

Similar praise came from another revered source, Adolph Zukor, the head of Paramount Pictures for half a century. Zukor felt that Bing's apparent lack of concern about troubles (in his film roles) had a way of infecting audiences with a kind of euphoria that helped make Bing a most welcome screen personality. He, too, testified that

---

* I can attest to that from my own experience. As the writer of a Television Easter Seal Special in Toronto of which Crosby was the star, I had occasion to work with him for several days. The changes he made in the script were all aimed at putting things into his own words, and he achieved that goal admirably. He was also a perfect gentleman to work with.

Crosby was absolutely reliable in his work habits. And Zukor and Capra both expressed admiration for Bing's photographic memory.

It has also been said of Crosby that he was always shrewd enough to insist on first-class supporting casts, and there is ample evidence to back this up. In his forty years of movie-making, he has worked with some of the strongest players in movies and they comprise an endless parade of friends, rivals, sidekicks, and foils—to say nothing of leading ladies.

It is doubtful if any other film star has appeared with such an impressive array of talented artists as Crosby has—and, more often than not, he worked with them in songs or comedy scenes that became priceless cinematic gems, lingering in the memory long after the films themselves have begun to dim.

Crosby's first feature film (after several short subjects) of any consequence was *The Big Broad-*

Double or Nothing. It was Mary Carlisle that Bing was in love with, but Martha Raye helped run the comedy department. (Paramount, 1937)

cast, made in 1932 with such stars as Burns and Allen, Kate Smith, the Mills Brothers, and the bands of Vincent Lopez and Cab Calloway. Crosby's contribution was largely restricted to singing two songs that were to become among his biggest hits: *Please* and *The Blue of the Night.*

In his next two features at Paramount, *College Humor* and *Too Much Harmony,* he was aided and abetted by Jack Oakie, that disarming cherub whose comedic prowess provided a nice balance to Bing's deadpan manner. Oakie, a master scene-stealer, often succeeded in upstaging Crosby, but the results were enjoyable movies and Bing was not one to care who got the laughs—so long as the laughs worked.

The following year, Crosby made *We're Not Dressing,* a movie musical very loosely based on Sir James Barrie's play, *The Admirable Crichton.* In this version, Crosby was an easygoing sailor working on heiress Carole Lombard's yacht. The passengers included Ethel Merman, Burns and Allen, Leon Errol, and a young Paramount contract player billed as Raymond Milland playing a snobbish wealthy Rival. As in the play, it was the lowly servant's ability to cope with life on a desert island that won him the respect and love of the high-born lady.

Lynne Overman, whose forlorn countenance was just this side of Ned Sparks's more famous sour look, was a welcome sidekick to Crosby in several films: *She Loves Me Not,* with Kitty Carlisle and Miriam Hopkins; *Two for Tonight,* with Joan Bennett; and *Dixie,* with Dorothy Lamour. (Sparks himself worked with Crosby in *Going Hollywood,* with Marion Davies," and *Too Much Harmony,* mentioned earlier.) And Charles Ruggles, another fine comedian of those days, worked with Bing in *The Big Broadcast of 1936* (which also had Jack Oakie and Burns and Allen) and *Anything Goes,* with Ethel Merman and Ida Lupino.

But one of Crosby's most memorable collaborations of that decade was with the redoubtable W. C. Fields in *Mississippi,* with Joan Bennett. This was based on a Booth Tarkington novel called *Magnolia,* and offered Fields as a boozy riverboat captain given to sharp practices and sharper retorts.

Some critics of the time regarded the movie as a shambles, mostly because all concerned gave

Waikiki Wedding. Leif Erikson (next to Shirley Ross) was Bing's humorless rival in this musical. (Paramount, 1937)

Dr. Rhythm. Beatrice Lillie never achieved the great following with film fans here that she had on the stage, but she enlivened this Crosby movie. (Paramount, 1938)

Fields too much leeway to indulge his bent for wild antics. But there can be no complaints about the priceless poker game scene in which Fields inadvertently dealt himself five aces and then tried to get rid of one of them.

Andy Devine, one of the most lovable of comic actors, was another Crosby favorite. The gravel-voiced, rotund Mr. Devine was in *Double or Nothing*, which had to do with an eccentric millionaire who scattered billfolds containing one hundred dollars and his card in them. The finders honest enough to return them were then given five thousand dollars each to invest and if they could double that money in a given time would inherit much more. Devine was a hobo, Crosby an out-of-work entertainer. They (along with Martha Raye) joined forces to invest their money in Crosby's dream: a night club.

The same year (1937) Bing starred in a bit of nonsense called *Waikiki Wedding* with Shirley Ross as his leading lady, the combined comedic talents of Bob Burns and Martha Raye—and a Bellamy-type "rival" in the person of Leif Erikson. Miss Ross was a pineapple heiress and Crosby was a press agent for her company. But the songs were pleasant, anyway.

Devine was also in *Dr. Rhythm*, tenuously based on O. Henry's tale, "The Badge of Policeman O'Roon." Devine played a sentimental zoo-

Dr. Rhythm. Andy Devine played a big-hearted zoo-keeper who decided to liberate all his charges. (Paramount, 1938)

keeper who got drunk and decided to liberate all the animals. Once again, great liberties were taken with the original story, but with such inspired comics as Devine, Sterling Holloway, and the inimitable Beatrice Lillie in the cast, there was fun galore.

Crosby had the considerable assistance of Mischa Auer in *East Side of Heaven*, with Joan Blondell as leading lady. Mischa played Bing's zany roommate and, as one reviewer put it, he "still maintained close cultural ties with a Russia that never existed."

Bob Burns, who later became known as "The Arkansas Traveller," was a Crosby sidekick in *Rhythm on the Range* and *Waikiki Wedding*, in both of which he and Martha Raye carried the comedy chores. In the latter, Leif Erikson served as Bing's stern-faced Rival.

Crosby got some substantial help from a couple of popular moppets as well. In *Pennies from Heaven*, little Edith Fellowes was around to give Bing a cozy avuncular air. And in *If I Had My Way*, young Gloria Jean helped Bing with the singing, and such stellar comics as Charles Winninger, El Brendel, and Allyn Joslyn were also featured.

In 1939, Crosby made a movie called *Paris Honeymoon*, with Shirley Ross as his American fiancée and Franciska Gaal as a simple European peasant girl who won his heart. But the comic highlights of the picture were provided by Akim Tamiroff, doing a wild take-off on the kind of sinister role he played in more dramatic movies of the time.

But Crosby's best film of the 1930s—and the first one in which critics were forced to take him a bit more seriously—was *Sing You Sinners*. (One critic, Archer Winsten of the *New York Post*, liked it so much he went back for another look and then gave it a second rave review.) Bing was the middle brother in this one, flanked by Fred MacMurray and young Donald O'Connor. Their widowed mother was Elizabeth Patterson. Sober Fred was engaged to Ellen Drew but couldn't afford to get married until loafer Bing got a job. (Shades of *The Irish in Us*, with Cagney and O'Brien.)

Instead of getting a steady job, however, Bing put his money on a nag, further compounding the family's economic problems. Besides having a

East Side of Heaven. The infant was called Baby Sandy, and the man bouncing him is the inimitable Mischa Auer. (Universal, 1939)

Rhythm on the Range. Bazooka player Bob Burns added his down-home humor to this musical about rodeo life. (Paramount, 1936)

If I Had My Way. Child star Gloria Jean was teamed with Crosby. One of their songs was "Meet the Sun Half Way." (Universal, 1940)

If I Had My Way. El Brendel, who relied on a Swedish accent, was Bing's funny friend here. (Universal, 1940)

Paris Honeymoon. Franciska Gaal was Bing's heroine and that veteran Funny Friend Edward Everett Horton was also on hand. (Paramount, 1939)

Paris Honeymoon. Dim-witted Ben Blue was an easy mark for con man Akim Tamiroff. (Paramount, 1939)

Sing You Sinners. Bing, Donald O'Connor, and Fred MacMurray were all brothers in this movie, and Ellen Drew was Fred's fianceé. (Paramount, 1938)

warm and reasonably intelligent script, the picture gave Crosby his meatiest role to date and also offered at least one memorable musical gem: Crosby, O'Connor, and MacMurray doing "Small Fry."

In *The Star Maker*, Crosby played the part of Gus Edwards, a real-life showman who specialized in working with children. Once again, Ned Sparks was on hand, as a child-hating press agent who was forced to play nursemaid to the kids, sometimes regaling them with wildly innacurate bedtime stories.

The following year, Bing and Mary Martin were teamed in *Rhythm on the River*, in which both of them were ghost writers for a phoney famous Broadway composer (smoothly played by Basil Rathbone) until they got together, compared notes, and decided they could manage nicely without him.

Crosby worked with Mary Martin again in 1941, in a film pretentiously titled *Birth of the Blues*. Among the supporting players were Brian Donlevy and Eddie ("Rochester") Anderson, and once you got over the foolish notion that the movie might really have some connection with the history of blues, there was plenty of good music to enjoy. Of special entertainment value was the trio of Crosby, Martin, and jazz ace Jack Tea-

The Star Maker. Sour-faced Ned Sparks was an ideal choice to play a child-hating theatrical agent in this fanciful biography of Gus Edwards. (Paramount, 1939)

Rhythm on the River. Basil Rathbone (here seen with Lillian Cornell) was a phony song writer who had two ghost writers: Bing Crosby and Mary Martin. (Paramount, 1940)

garden singing "The Waiter, The Porter, and the Upstairs Maid."

In 1942 came one of Crosby's biggest hits and a happy collaboration with another of the great musical comedy superstars, Fred Astaire. This was *Holiday Inn,* and besides the fun of Bing and Fred competing for girls there was the introduction of Irving Berlin's timeless hit, "White Christmas."

Bing's teaming with Astaire was successful enough that it was repeated—but not until five years had gone by—in yet another film with songs by Irving Berlin. This was called *Blue Skies,* and although it didn't have as noteworthy a score as *Holiday Inn* it was a huge box-office success, grossing some six million dollars the year it was issued.

During the war years, most of the major film studios turned out big, glossy, star-laden flag-waving musicals—ostentatious evidence of the industry's "war effort." Paramount's was called

Star Spangled Rhythm and Crosby appeared in it, along with Ray Milland, Bob Hope, Mary Martin, Fred MacMurray, Dick Powell, Dorothy Lamour, Betty Hutton, Veronica Lake, Vera Zorina, and others. Crosby sang in front of a replica of Mount Rushmore.

One of Bing's lesser efforts in 1943 was *Dixie,* a "biography" of the Civil War era minstrel Dan Emmett. Apart from the fact that Emmett wrote the song "Dixie," the film bore little resemblance to his life, and despite the presence of Dorothy Lamour, Marjorie Reynolds, and Billy DeWolfe, not much about the picture was memorable.

The following year, Crosby again took note of World War Two in a service comedy called *Here Come the Waves.* This one offered Betty Hutton in a dual role, playing twin sisters who were both WAVES. Crosby and Sonny Tufts kept getting them mixed up, and the film also had the added attraction of Bing doing a broad take-off on the then current appeal of "swoon singer" Frank Sinatra.

But it was another 1944 film that brought Bing Crosby his greatest laurels. Donning a clerical collar for the first time, Bing played a casual, golf-playing priest who became a thorn in the side of crusty Barry Fitzgerald in Leo McCarey's *Going My Way.* (Note, incidentally, how such personal interests of Crosby's as golf and horse playing work their way into his films.) The team-

Birth of the Blues. Brian Donlevy was really no match for Bing in Mary Martin's eyes. (Paramount, 1941)

177

Holiday Inn. The ladies with Crosby and Astaire are Marjorie Reynolds and Virginia Dale, one for each. (Paramount, 1942)

ing of Crosby and Fitzgerald was an inspired one and the film not only proved a box-office bonanza but went on to win seven Academy Awards, including one each for Fathers Bing and Barry.

Nor were its musical delights skimpy. Besides "teaching" a bunch of kids to sing "Swinging On A Star," there was the touching rendering of "Too-ra-loo-ra-loo-ra" before the bedridden Fitzgerald. And for drama there was the moving moment when opera star Rise Stevens, encountering Crosby after a long dormant romance, realizes that he has become a priest.

Bing's reversed collar came in handy several more times. McCarey followed up *Going My Way* with the equally successful *Bells of St. Mary's*, in which Father Bing had a tender, sensitive (but irreproachable) relationship with a heavenly Ingrid Bergman, as a nun. The movie and Miss Bergman both received Oscar nominations but missed out on the awards.

Nor could Bing resist working with Barry Fitzgerald again. In *Welcome Stranger*, Crosby was the young doctor sent to help the aging country doctor—Fitzgerald. As in *Going My Way*, the older man resented the breezy, seemingly incompetent upstart, but it all worked out fine in the end.

They tried it one more time, in *Top of the Morning*, with predictably diminishing returns. This time, Bing was a United States insurance investigator in Ireland trying to solve the theft of the Blarney Stone and Fitzgerald was a grouchy old Civil Guard constable with a fine Irish thirst and Ann Blyth for a daughter.

(Bing played a priest one more time, in 1959, in *Say One for Me*, which had Debbie Reynolds, Robert Wagner, and Ray Walston in the cast—and not too much else to recommend it.)

But Bing didn't devote all his time to working with Barry Fitzgerald. In 1948, Billy Wilder, one of Hollywood's most gifted comedy directors, had Bing Crosby and Joan Fontaine in a delight-ful film called *The Emperor Waltz*. Bing played a phonograph salesman on the loose in Franz-Josef's empire, trying to sell him this newfangled gadget. In the cast were Richard Haydn as the emperor and Sig Ruman as his overbearing vet, named "Dr. Zweiback."

The following year, Crosby turned to a famous American author again: Mark Twain. He starred in *A Connecticut Yankee in King Arthur's Court*, with Rhonda Fleming, Sir Cedric Hardwicke, and for laughs, William Bendix.

Then came his fruitful association with Frank

Here Come the WAVES. There were two of them (both played by Betty Hutton) so Bing and Sonny Tufts were able to stop scrapping. (Paramount, 1944)

Capra, which yielded two successful films. First was *Riding High,* a remake of an old Capra success called *Broadway Bill.* It dealt with horse racing, and the good cast included Charles Bickford, Colleen Gray, and William Demarest, more or less filling the spot Lynne Overman had occupied in earlier Crosby pictures.

After that, Capra directed Crosby again in *Here Comes the Groom,* in which Bing picked up two French orphans and then realized he had to get married in order to keep them. Jane Wyman was the bride he settled on, and Franchot Tone was the millionaire playboy (what else?) he had to compete with.

He did another film with Jane Wyman in 1952, titled *Just for You.* But even with Ethel Barrymore in the cast, this one didn't have as much appeal as the Capra effort.

In 1954, Crosby turned serious actor again in *The Country Girl,* based on a Clifford Odets play. Starring with him were Grace Kelly and William Holden. Crosby played an alcoholic entertainer whose weakness has chained his wife to him, and Holden was the director who came between them. Miss Kelly won an Oscar and Bing won his second New York Film Critics award.

Then he returned to musicals again and turned out two whoppers. *White Christmas* teamed him

Going My Way. Flanking opera star Rise Stevens are two Oscar winners: Barry Fitzgerald and Bing Crosby. (Paramount, 1944)

The Bells of St. Mary's. A priest again, this time with Ingrid Bergman as an ailing nun. (RKO, 1945)

Top o' the Morning. The Crosby-Fitzgerald combination worked again, though perhaps not as successfully as at first. (Paramount, 1949)

Say One for Me. Bing's clerical collar came in handy once more to straighten out an erring Robert Wagner. (20th Century-Fox, 1959)

A Connecticut Yankee. William Bendix joined the festivities in this version of the Mark Twain story starring Bing. (Paramount, 1949)

Here Comes the Groom. The bride was Jane Wyman, the loser was Franchot Tone, and the groom was Bing. (Paramount, 1951)

with Danny Kaye and emerged as the biggest box-office success Crosby was ever in. It made twelve million dollars, and in those days of relatively uninflated ticket prices (1954) only a handful of films of any kind had ever done better.

Somewhat less successful (but still a big hit) was *High Society,* an updated musical version of *The Philadelphia Story,* with Bing as the irreverent first husband of Grace Kelly and Frank Sinatra and Celeste Holm in the roles first played by James Stewart and Ruth Hussey. Louis Armstrong was also thrown in as a musical plus.

Apart from the tender Crosby-Kelly duet, "True Love," the wondrous clowning of Crosby and Sinatra. proved irresistible, as in the song "A Swell Party."

One more "big" musical was made in 1956. This was a new edition of the Cole Porter show, *Anything Goes,* but even though it had Crosby reteamed with Donald O'Connor, plus Mitzi Gaynor and Jeanmaire, it failed to approach the popular success of the earlier efforts.

Crosby played more serious roles in *Little Boy Lost* and *Man on Fire,* with moderate success, and teamed with Fabian and Tuesday Weld in something called *High Time,* which had to do with a middle-aged man returning to school. In *Robin and the Seven Hoods,* he romped with

Dean Martin and Frank Sinatra, proving only that he was still a good entertainer. And he did justice to the role of the drunken old doctor (first played by Thomas Mitchell) in an otherwise inferior remake of *Stagecoach.*

That pretty well covers the Crosby film years, with one major and delicious exception, and that has been purposely left for last.

Beginning in 1941 and ending in 1962, Bing Crosby was fifty percent of the zaniest, wildest, most irrepressible on-again-off-again musical comedy team in Hollywood history. The other half was Bob Hope.

Unlikely though it may seem, legend has it that the first in this unorthodox series, *The Road to Singapore,* was originally intended for Fred MacMurray and George Burns. (Would that have meant Gracie Allen in a sarong?) When MacMurray rejected it, the way was paved for Crosby and Hope.

The combination clicked from the very beginning, largely because the chemistry between the two stars worked. They enjoyed clowning with each other, trading insults, ad libbing all manner of nonsense. They had done this on radio shows and simply continued it in their movies.

The writers of *The Road to Singapore* were both highly respected Hollywood craftsmen: Don Hartman, who later became head of production at Paramount, and Frank Butler, who had written

The Country Girl. Crosby in a dramatic role, with Grace Kelly and William Holden. (Paramount, 1954)

High Society. An updated musical version of *The Philadelphia Story* with Bing, Grace Kelly, and Frank Sinatra. (MGM, 1957)

countless comedies, including *College Humor,* one of Crosby's first pictures. At first, both they and the director (Victor Schertzinger) were stunned by the liberties Crosby and Hope were taking with the script. (Once when the writers visited the set, Hope called out to them: "If you recognize anything of yours, yell 'Bingo!'") Crosby and Hope also got Paramount to hire Barney Dean, an old vaudeville comic buddy, to hang around the set and toss in ideas for gags.

Somehow, the breezy "feud" between Hope and Crosby worked and the movie was a refreshing hit. The studio was encouraged to do more, and

Bing and Bob were encouraged to do more ad libbing.

The "plots" were fragile and hokey. Crosby and Hope were simply two down-and-out adventurers forever getting into scrapes and fighting, faking, or gagging their way out of them. The third element was the ever-present Dorothy Lamour as a mock damsel in distress.

Crosby and Hope did their patty-cake routine, which invariably ended with both of them socking whatever hulking menace was blocking their escape.

As the series of pictures progressed, more and

184

more rules went out the window. Crosby, in a "romantic" scene with Lamour, kidded the Hollywood cliché of the sudden sound of an unseen symphony orchestra when the hero was about to sing. Then he leaned out of the canoe they were in, rippled his hand through the water and —presto!—a harp arpeggio followed by full orchestra to accompany his song.

Hope broke another hallowed convention, this one against stepping out of character and talking directly into the camera, delivering an aside. It didn't matter; the jokes worked.

From Singapore to Zanzibar to Morocco to Utopia to Rio to Bali—on and on they went, kibbitzing, cutting up, brawling, singing, tricking each other to get close to Lamour, ignoring all logic, effecting miraculous escapes against ridiculous odds.

They were two playboys who fled to Singapore to forget women; they were carnival hustlers in darkest Africa and poked fun at safari movies; they were broken-down vaudevillians in Bali, fending off an assortment of savages; they went to Alaska for gold but found Lamour; they ran wild in South America.

And all Roads led to the bank, as moviegoers

Anything Goes. Donald O'Connor, whose career in films was launched in a Crosby movie (*Sing You Sinners*) in 1938, was Bing's co-star eighteen years later in this musical. (Paramount, 1956)

Road to Morocco. Wherever the road took them, Crosby always managed to outsmart Hope. (Paramount, 1942)

continued to enjoy the peripatetic antics of Bing and Bob. Over the space of a dozen years, they made six of these mad "Road" pictures, and the only inviolable rule was that Crosby always ended up with the girl (always Dorothy Lamour) and Hope with the last laugh.

In 1962, nine years after *The Road to Bali*, the sixth in the series, Crosby and Hope teamed up once more for *The Road to Hong Kong.* This was the only one of the "Road" pictures not made for Paramount. Dorothy Lamour was in it, but only briefly. And despite the presence in the cast of Peter Sellers, Joan Collins, and Robert Morley, the picture didn't turn out as

well as most of the others—nor was it a box-office success. Perhaps the "Road" had been traveled too often and grown too bumpy.

But while the series lasted, Crosby had the assistance of Hollywood's most engaging loser in Bob Hope, and the two of them—with Lamour as an added attraction—comprised one of the most popular musical comedy teams Hollywood has ever produced.

Jack Oakie, W. C. Fields, Fred Astaire, Donald O'Connor, Danny Kaye, Barry Fitzgerald, Frank Sinatra, Bob Hope—nobody but Crosby has been blessed with such a parade of film friends, foes, and foils.

The Road to Zanzibar. Hope and Crosby as a couple of hustlers ran into difficulties in Africa. (Paramount, 1941)

The Road to Rio. The bellhops were an act called the Wiere Brothers. The other two guys you know. (Paramount, 1947)

The Road to Utopia. Bing, Dottie, and Bob aged handsomely in this one, as did the series. (Paramount, 1945)

The Road to Hong Kong. A late addition to the series,
this one was somewhat less successful than the others.
(United Artists, 1962)

7
Ralph Bellamy Reborn

The time lapse between *The Awful Truth* and *Pillow Talk* was just twenty-two years. The first movie, teaming Irene Dunne and Cary Grant, began a cycle of light romantic comedies in which Cary Grant or Fred MacMurray or Melvyn Douglas pursued Irene Dunne or Carole Lombard or Rosalind Russell, occasionally bumping into an obstacle like Ralph Bellamy or Ray Milland or Robert Young.

Pillow Talk, made in 1959, was the first of a "new" cycle of romantic comedies to team Doris Day with Rock Hudson. Miss Day, the Irene Dunne of this era, went on to make more such films, with Hudson, Grant, James Garner, and others.

The biggest single change in those two decades was the cutting down of the distance between the camera and the bedroom. Miss Day remained as pure as Miss Dunne. (Oscar Levant once claimed: "I knew Doris Day before she was a virgin.") Hudson and Garner were as determined to take Doris to bed as Grant and MacMurray had been in their films. Their methods may have varied, but not their goals.

Another factor that has remained constant is the role of the Other Man. Ralph Bellamy, Don Ameche, and Eddie Albert are, naturally, playing older parts. Jack Carson, George Sanders, and Franchot Tone are dead, as are Robert Benchley, Charles Butterworth, Mischa Auer, and some of the other talented and personable actors who helped make those comedies work.

But a new generation—if not a new breed—of Other Men has come along to fill the gap. Many of them are as adroit at playing the third part of the triangle as were the Bellamys, Carsons, and Millands. Some have already moved up from Other Men roles to full stardom.

Before surveying these new Bellamys, however, it seems worthwhile to take note of a few of the most stalwart Other Men of the "older" generation who, somehow, managed to keep right on going twenty and twenty-five years after they first began attracting attention, still filling out triangles.

Foremost among them is David Niven, who first presented a challenge of sorts to Gary Cooper in *Bluebeard's Eighth Wife*, in 1938. Nineteen years later, in *The Little Hut*, he was still the middle-man with Stewart Granger and Ava Gardner. And it didn't end there. Niven was still a convincing and delightful Rival in *Bedtime Story*. This was in 1964—six years after he had won an Academy Award in *Separate Tables* as an aging phoney major given to pinching women he sat next to in cinemas.

Bedtime Story, a good comedy that just barely avoided the borderline of questionable taste, pitted Niven against Marlon Brando, the latter in a rare comedy role.

The Little Hut. Two decades after first establishing an identity, David Niven was still playing would-be home wrecker, in this case with Ava Gardner and Stewart Granger. (MGM, 1957)

Both played unscrupulous fortune-hunters in a constant game of one-upmanship, a duel of wits and trickery to relieve Shirley Jones of her money. (It turns out she doesn't have any, but that's beside the point.) When Brando poses as a paralyzed soldier, confined to a wheelchair not by any injury but by an emotional disturbance based on rejection by women, the naive Miss Jones offers herself to him and even writes to a famous psychiatrist (invented by Brando) begging him to help Brando. Niven then masquerades as the fictitious "Dr. Schaffenhausen" and subjects Brando to a series of cruel tests (whacking Brando's legs with a riding crop, tickling his feet) in the presence of Miss Jones, knowing the "paralyzed soldier" must bear the tortures or reveal himself as a fraud. In the end, Brando marries Miss Jones (not what he originally had in mind) and Niven is left to prey on other wealthy women, free of Brando's competition.

Also in the 1960s, Niven (who was born in 1909) appeared opposite Doris Day in *Please Don't Eat the Daisies,* played a clever jewel thief in *The Pink Panther,* parodied the David Niven rival role in *Ask Any Girl* with Shirley MacLaine, did a mock spy thriller called *Where the Spies*

Bedtime Story. Veteran rival David Niven is startled at Marlon Brando's tantrum. The unidentified lady at right was merely one of Niven's and Brando's targets. (Universal, 1964)

Are, got back into an officer's uniform for *Fifty Five Days at Peking* and *The Guns of Navarone*, and played Sir James Bond in *Casino Royale*. And just to keep from being idle, he also appeared in the television series "The Rogues."

Another Rival of impressive staying power was Robert Cummings. He was playing Other Man roles in the middle 1930s, then went on to leading roles for more than a decade, after which he moved into television for a considerable period of time.

But in the 1960s he was back in movies, playing only a slightly older version of earlier Cummings types. In *What a Way To Go* (1963) he was one of a small army of men who vied for Shirley MacLaine. Others were Paul Newman, Dick Van Dyke, Robert Mitchum, Gene Kelly, and Dean Martin. He also appeared with Miss MacLaine and Yves Montand in another comedy in the early 1960s titled *My Geisha*. In 1964, Cummings played a less sympathetic role in *The Carpetbaggers*, which had Alan Ladd, Carroll Baker, and George Peppard as stars. And in 1966, he supported Warren Beatty and Leslie Caron, playing a wealthy bachelor in *Promise Her Anything*. The same year he was in the remake of

My Man Godfrey. Remakes are rarely as good as originals, and this one was no exception, even with David Niven and June Allyson. (Universal, 1957)

Stagecoach, playing a crooked and cowardly banker.

Other actors well established before the 1960s turned effectively to Other Men roles during that decade. Jack Lemmon had become a big star in the 1950s, appearing in Judy Holliday comedies and in such diverse items as *Fire Down Below* and *Bell, Book, and Candle.* Then, in the mid-1960s, he played a mock villain in Blake Edwards's farce, *The Great Race,* with Tony Curtis as the "hero." Dean Martin was a Friend/Rival in *Marriage on the Rocks,* with Frank Sinatra and Deborah Kerr, in 1965. Louis Jourdan came briefly between Elizabeth Taylor and Richard Burton in *The V.I.P.'s.* And Fred MacMurray, who had spent a lifetime taking ladies away from virtually every Rival in Hollywood history, finally lost (Shirley MacLaine) to Jack Lemmon in *The Apartment.* Maurice Chevalier, aged about seventy-five at the time, was a kind of rival to young Horst Buchholtz for Leslie Caron in *Fanny.*

Between the older generation of Other Men and the newer contenders, one actor stands out as a kind of bridge. He is Gig Young.

He was a late bloomer, for although he was appearing in movies since 1941, his name was not generally known to the public until many years later.

That first year, he was in *The Gay Sisters,* which starred Barbara Stanwyck and George Brent, but hardly anyone noticed. In 1943, he was briefly a plaything for Bette Davis in *Old Acquaintance,* but she magnanimously yielded him to a younger girl. He was involved in a soapy mess called *Escape Me Never* in 1947, with Errol Flynn and Eleanor Parker as stars.

Then, as it must to all Hollywood Other Men, rejection by Joan Crawford came to Gig Young in 1953, when she chose Michael Wilding over him in *Torch Song.* But in *You for Me,* he played a struggling young doctor who won Jane Greer away from Peter Lawford.

By 1958, he was fairly well established as a Rival/Nice Friend, as in *Teacher's Pet,* with Clark Gable and Doris Day, and *Tunnel of Love,* with Doris Day and Richard Widmark.

By the 1960s his experience at losing gracefully came in handy when a new cycle of light romantic comedies began to pick up steam. Young was sort of an American Niven, a latter-day Tone. He was either the hero's half-sober friend or ineffectual rival.

One of his best roles was in *That Touch of Mink,* made in 1962, with Cary Grant and Doris Day. Grant played a slick tycoon bent on conquering the virtuous Miss Day. Young was Grant's boozing financial adviser, a lip-service lib-

Ask Any Girl. Shirley MacLaine, alone in the big city, meets such wolves as Gig Young and David Niven. (MGM, 1959)

The Carpetbaggers. Robert Cummings turned smooth-talking villain in this box office hit. That's Martha Hyer with him. (Paramount, 1964)

Fire Down Below. Rita Hayworth was the cause of friction between Robert Mitchum and Jack Lemmon in this action film. (Columbia, 1954)

The Great Race. Jack Lemmon was a flamboyant mock villain in this comedy, with Tony Curtis and Natalie Wood as lovers. (Warner Brothers, 1966)

Marriage on the Rocks. Dean Martin "accidentally" got married to Deborah Kerr in Mexico. The real hero was Frank Sinatra. (Warner Brothers, 1965)

The V.I.P.'s. Louis Jourdan almost convinced Elizabeth Taylor to run away with him but she finally returned to Richard Burton. (MGM, 1963)

The Apartment. Fred MacMurray, who spent a life-time beating off all opposition, finally lost Shirley MacLaine to Jack Lemmon. (United Artists, 1960)

Fanny. Veteran star Maurice Chevalier was an unusual but charming other man in this film. Leslie Caron played the title role. (Warner Brothers, 1961)

Young at Heart. In this remake of *Four Daughters,* Frank Sinatra had the John Garfield role, but he wasn't killed off. He lived and beat out Gig Young for the girl. (Warner Brothers, 1955)

Tunnel of Love. Gig Young with Gia Scala, the second leads in this Doris Day-Richard Widmark comedy. (MGM, 1958)

eral who blames Grant for corrupting him with a high-paying job. In one scene, Young confides to his psychoanalyst: "I still haven't heard from my mother. Not that it bothers me. But it's been two days."

A year later, in *For Love Or Money*, he was Kirk Douglas's friend (Funny) and the leading lady was Mitzi Gaynor. And in 1965, Young was with Rock Hudson and Gina Lollobrigida in a comedy called *Strange Bedfellows*, this time trying to patch up Hudson's shaky marriage.

Young's long career had some duds, as well. They included an English melodrama, *The Shuttered Room*, a pointless comedy with Shirley Jones titled *A Ticklish Affair*, and even the indignity of playing second banana to Elvis Presley in a remake of *Kid Gallahad*.

But in 1970, he won an Academy Award as the best actor of the year in *They Shoot Horses*

Don't They—which wasn't even a comedy.

If Gig Young was the bridge from old to new Other Men, then Tony Randall is virtually the reincarnation of the Bellamy-Carson-Cummings character.

Randall first won acclaim on television as the friend of "Mr. Peepers" in the excellent series of that name. His first good film role was in *Oh Men! Oh Women!,* in which he played an unhinged patient of psychoanalyst David Niven. His comedic talents were apparent in that film and also in *Will Success Spoil Rock Hunter,* in which he starred opposite Jayne Mansfield. He was an eccentric income tax investigator in *The Mating Game,* with Debbie Reynolds and Paul Douglas, in 1959.

That same year, he turned true-blue Bellamy in *Pillow Talk,* with Doris Day and Rock Hudson. This updated boy-chases-girl comedy had Randall as a superfluous Rival who patently doesn't stand a chance.

In one scene, Randall is driving a tearful Doris Day back to New York after Hudson has upset her. They stop at a roadside café for coffee, where two truck drivers take a dim view of the innocent Randall and his crying female companion. When Miss Day's tears begin to get out of control (a must in any Doris Day film) Randall slaps her face to snap her out of it and earns himself a beating by the chivalrous truck drivers.

Next was *Lover Come Back,* again with Randall as the third part of a triangle. This time the battleground for Rock and Doris was the advertising agency business and the script allowed for some broad swipes at that massive target. As usual, Randall stole the laughs every chance he had.

In 1964, the picture was *Send Me No Flowers,* and besides the Day-Hudson combination, it offered a fine trio of Other Men roles. Hudson, who believed himself dying, was determined to arrange his widow's future. Randall played his tipsy, sentimental friend; Clint Walker (of the "Cheyenne" television series) was Hudson's choice for Doris's second husband—and turned out to be an insufferable bore; and Paul Lynde was an over-eager cemetery plot salesman.

Curiously, when Randall was moved up to leading roles he was less successful. He was with Barbara Eden and Burl Ives in *The Brass Bottle* (1964), with Shirley Jones in *Fluffy* (1965), and

That Touch of Mink. Cary Grant and Doris Day were the stars, but many of the laughs came from Gig Young in a real Bellamy role. (Universal, 1962)

The Shuttered Room. One of Gig Young's lesser efforts. With him above is Carol Lynley. (Warner Brothers, 1968)

arriving in New York to visit him. She and Taylor meet, get caught in the rain and go to Robertson's apartment, finding it unoccupied. When Culp (her small-town fiancé) arrives, Taylor is forced to masquerade as Jane's brother. And when Robertson turns up, the confusion is compounded. All hands proved skillful in this comedy, but Culp's stuffy square was reminiscent of the Bellamy roles.

Chuck Connors, star of television's "The Rifleman," became a handy Other Man in some films. He was in *Designing Woman*, with Gregory Peck and Lauren Bacall. Then that old standby, *My Favorite Wife*, was dusted off and reshaped into a Doris Day film called *Move Over Darling*. This time, Doris returned from the dead (along with Chuck, her desert island companion) in time to find her husband (James Garner) about to remarry.

Bang, Bang, You're Dead, with Senta Berger and Terry-Thomas, in 1966. None of these gave Randall much opportunity to further enhance his reputation for comedy playing.

And then television, where he'd first made his name, came up with a plum: with Jack Klugman, Randall was cast in the series based on Neil Simon's hit play and movie, *The Odd Couple*. It proved to be one of the best situation comedy series of its time.

Gig Young and Tony Randall became the most successful Other Men of the 1960s, but they didn't have the whole field to themselves.

Robert Culp (after his "I Spy" series with Bill Cosby but before playing the lead in *Bob and Carol and Ted and Alice*) turned in a good Bellamy-type performance in *Sunday in New York*, a 1964 comedy with Jane Fonda, Rod Taylor, and Cliff Robertson.

In this one, Miss Fonda was Robertson's sister,

The Mating Game. Tony Randall and Debbie Reynolds starred in this one, aided by Paul Douglas and Fred Clark. (MGM, 1959)

Will Success Spoil Rock Hunter? This comedy helped establish Tony Randall, here with Jayne Mansfield and Joan Blondell. (20th Century-Fox, 1957)

David Janssen, another television star, played a Rival in *My Six Loves* (1963), with Debbie Reynolds and Cliff Robertson.

Before Robertson graduated to leads, he served his apprenticeship in a succession of lesser roles, from Henry Fonda's political foe in *The Best Man* to *Gidget*, with Sandra Dee. He was even Rex Harrison's clever aide in *The Honey Pot*.

Robert Wagner, whose career in films goes back to the early 1950s, got a new lease on life with his television series, "It Takes a Thief," then turned up in a good Rival role in the 1969 film, *Winning*, with Paul Newman and Joanne Woodward.

Robert Redford, who has since become a top-rated box-office star, paid his dues via a number

of supporting roles. He was the escaped convict returning home in *The Chase*, with Marlon Brando, Angie Dickinson, and Jane Fonda. He was Natalie Wood's homosexual husband in *Inside Daisy Clover*. And he was in *War Hunt*, a serious Korean War film that also starred John Saxon.

The Chase also had James Fox in its cast, in the role of the man Jane Fonda had fallen in love with while Redford was in prison. Fox had a comedic Other Man role in *Those Magnificent Men in Their Flying Machines*, with Stuart Whitman as hero and Sarah Miles as the prize. He was a sympathetic second lead to George Segal in *King Rat* and a menacing villain in *The Servant*, with Dirk Bogarde.

Pillow Talk. A typical Randall moment. He slaps Doris Day to snap her out of her hysteria and a truck driver socks him. (Universal, 1959)

James Coburn, who symbolized (along with Lee Marvin) the "new" craggy, tough hero in his later films, worked his way up from a smaller role in *The Great Escape*, a hoodlum in *Charade*, with Cary Grant and Audrey Hepburn, and an excellent Funny Friend role in *The Americanization of Emily*, with Julie Andrews and James Garner.

The realm of Funny Friends has produced some impressive successors to the Jack Oakies, Mischa Auers, and Edward Everett Hortons.

One of the most successful has been Paul Lynde, mentioned earlier in connection with *Send Me No Flowers.* Lynde also contributed sterling performances in *Under the Yum Yum Tree*, with Jack Lemmon; *The Glass Bottom Boat*, with Doris Day and Richard Harris; and *How Sweet It Is*, with Debbie Reynolds and James Garner.

Carl Reiner, gifted both as actor and writer, was an excellent Friend/Rival in *The Gazebo*, a 1960 comedy with Glenn Ford and Debbie Reynolds. He was also in *The Thrill of It All*, with Doris Day and James Garner. Reiner then played a leading role in *The Russians Are Coming, The Russians Are Coming*, which also had Alan Arkin, Paul Ford, and other gifted comics.

Dick Van Dyke, long a success on television, emerged as a good film comic, in Friend/Rival roles (*The Art of Love*, with James Garner) as

Lover Come Back. The Rock Hudson-Doris Day comedies were often aided by the presence of Tony Randall. (Universal, 1962)

well as in leading roles, as in *Cold Turkey.*

And George C. Scott, one of the top stars today, has ranged from heavy (*The Hustler*) to Rival (*Not With My Wife, You Don't*) to comic gangster (*The Yellow Rolls Royce*).

Other effective Funny Friends and mock villains to emerge in the 1960s—some of whom have since become stars—include Walter Matthau, Peter Falk, Elliott Gould, Donald Sutherland, Gene Wilder, Jack Weston, Jack Gilford, and Terry-Thomas, not to mention George Segal, Burt Reynolds, Gene Hackman, and Peter Boyle.

Movie styles have changed substantially, of course, from the 1930s—just as American values and mores have. It's a long, long way from *The*

Last of Mrs. Cheyney to *The Last Tango in Paris.* Heroes are less perfect; heroines are less demure; scripts are more "adult" and dialogue is infinitely more candid. So-called production codes have more or less kept pace with changing moral standards, and pressure groups are less influential—at least with regard to matters sexual.

But the functions of the Other Man in Hollywood movies still remain essentially the same: to complete the triangle, to offer some laughs, to make the hero look good—and the movie look better.

And just as the Ralph Bellamys, Jack Carsons, Don Ameches, and Cesar Romeros fulfilled those functions in the 1930s and 1940s, the Gig Youngs,

Tony Randalls, and Paul Lyndes served to perpetuate this honored tradition in later decades.

As in the past, no movie fan pays his money at the box office because of the presence in the cast of actors who play Other Men. But most movie fans get more pleasure from the movies because of the talents and personalities of those actors.

Send Me No Flowers. Besides Rock and Doris, this one had Tony Randall as a Funny Friend and Clint Walker as a square suitor. (Universal, 1964)

Sunday in New York. Jane Fonda got involved with Rod Taylor and had difficulty in getting funny fianceé Robert Culp to understand. (MGM, 1964)

Designing Woman. Despite the indignity Gregory Peck suffers at the hands of Chuck Connors, it was Peck who won Lauren Bacall. (MGM, 1957)

The Lady Takes a Flyer. Jeff Chandler (center) and Lana Turner were the stars, and Chuck Connors was a friend. The nurse is Pat McMahon. (Universal, 1958)

My Six Loves. Debbie Reynolds fell for clergyman Cliff Robertson, leaving David Janssen as odd man out. (Paramount, 1962)

The Interns. Among the upcoming actors in this one were Cliff Robertson, Michael Callan, and James MacArthur, seen above. (Columbia, 1962)

The Best Man. This political story had Henry Fonda and Cliff Robertson as foes, plus Gene Raymond and Kevin McCarthy in supporting roles. (United Artists, 1964)

The Honey Pot. Cliff Robertson was friend to Rex Harrison in this sly comedy which also had Susan Hayward, Maggie Smith, and Edie Adams. (United Artists, 1967)

The Mountain. Spencer Tracy and Robert Wagner were mountain-climbing brothers, with Wagner as the un-nice one. (Paramount, 1956)

Winning. Rival Robert Wagner guzzles champagne while Paul Newman kisses the beauty queen. Newman won it all. (Universal, 1969)

The Chase. Marlon Brando was the honest Southern sheriff and Robert Redford the young escaped convict returning home. (Columbia, 1966)

Inside Daisy Clover. Despite that clinch, Natalie Wood and Robert Redford were not fated to stay together in this film. (Warner Brothers, 1966)

Those Magnificent Men in Their Flying Machines. James Fox lost both the race and the girl (Sarah Miles, sipping champagne) to Stuart Whitman. (20th Century-Fox, 1965)

211

King Rat. George Segal, left, was the soldier expert at surviving in a prison camp, James Fox his devoted friend. (Columbia, 1965)

The Americanization of Emily. James Coburn was a loud Navy type in this fine antiwar comedy that starred James Garner and Julie Andrews. Also above is William Windom. (MGM, 1967)

Charade. The stars were Cary Grant and Audrey Hepburn, the film also had James Coburn as a heavy. At left is veteran character actor Ned Glass. (Universal, 1964)

Send Me No Flowers. The new generation of Funny Friend is represented here by Paul Lynde, with Rock Hudson. (Universal, 1964)

213

The Gazebo. Glenn Ford had Debbie Reynolds as wife and Carl Reiner as friend/rival in this comedy. (MGM, 1960)

The Art of Love. Television's Dick Van Dyke and James Garner were at odds in this comedy romance. (Universal, 1965)

The Russians Are Coming, The Russians Are Coming. Carl Reiner and Alan Arkin headed a cast of comedy players for this highly successful film. Half-hidden by Arkin is John Phillip Law, and the girl is Eva Marie Saint. (United Artists, 1966)

The Yellow Rolls Royce. George C. Scott was a comic gangster whose girl, Shirley MacLaine, had a brief fling with Alain Delon before returning to Scott. (MGM, 1965)

Island of Love. Robert Preston had the help of two gifted comedians here: Walter Matthau and Tony Randall. (Warner Brothers, 1963)

The Incredible Mr. Limpet. Jack Weston was Don Knotts's funny rival in this comedy. With him above is Carole Cook. (Warner Brothers, 1964)

A *Pocketful of Miracles*. Peter Falk strikes a Columbo-like pose in this scene with Glenn Ford. (United Artists, 1961)

Please Don't Eat the Daisies. David Niven, Janis Paige, and Jack Weston in a scene from the Doris Day film. (MGM, 1960)

Where Were You When the Lights Went Out? That's gap-toothed Terry-Thomas on the floor with Doris Day, and Robert Morse glowering at them. (MGM, 1968)

Who's Afraid of Virginia Woolf? Elizabeth Taylor and Richard Burton battled royally, aided by George Segal and (hidden) Sandy Dennis. (Warner Brothers, 1966)

*M*A*S*H.* Donald Sutherland and Elliott Gould zoomed to stardom in this irreverent antiwar comedy. (20th Century-Fox, 1969)

Oh Men! Oh Women! Two generations of Other Men face to face: Tony Randall and David Niven. (20th Century-Fox, 1957)

Index